101 ITEMS TO SELL ON EBAY

How to Make Money Selling Garage Sale & Thrift Store Finds!

By Ann Eckhart

Eighth Edition

To my dad, thank you for your
unconditional love and support!

TABLE OF CONTENTS

#39 Furs

#40 Graphing Calculators

#41 Hand-Held Electronic Games

#42 Hallmark Ornaments

#43 Harry Potter Hardcover Books

#44 Hawaiian Shirts

#45 Hockey Memorabilia

#46 Holly Hobbie

#47 Home Based/Direct Sales Merchandise

#48 Hot Rollers

#49 Hymnals

#50 JCPenney and Sears Catalogs

#51 John Deere Collectibles

#52 Jordan Era Chicago Bulls Memorabilia

#53 Keurig Coffee Makers

#54 Little House on the Prairie Books

#55 London Fog Trench Coats

#56 Matchbooks

#57 NCAA Sports Memorabilia

#58 Norman Rockwell Figurines

#79 Sony Walkmans

#80 Starbucks Coffee Mugs

#81 Starter Brand Sports Jackets

#82 Tervis Tumblers

#83 Thermos Stanley Containers from Aladdin

#84 Thomas the Train

#85 Tommy Bahama Clothing

#86 Travel Tin Plates

#87 Tube Radios

#88 TV Show Coffee Mugs

#89 TV Show DVD/Blu-Ray Boxed Sets

#90 Typewriter Keys

#91 UGGS

#92 Vests

#93 Victoria's Secret Bags

#94 Vintage Cameras

#95 Vintage Camera Film & Flash Bulbs

#96 Vintage Dohoney & Bourke

#97 Vintage Portable Typewriters

#98 Watkins Ceramic Pie Plates

INTRODUCTION

In 2005, I left my nine-to-five office job to start a home-based gift basket business. My dream had been to open a brick-and-mortar gift shop; but research told me that only 1% of independently owned specialty stores survive past their first year. Only 1%! I had to accept the fact that most boutiques are hobby businesses, not big income earners. However, home-based gift basket businesses had a much higher success rate, so I launched Annabella's Gift Baskets from my home.

I had developed a long list of business contacts from my years working for the local Chamber of Commerce, so I had a good foundation of customers to start with. And while I was busy for the first part of the year, by summer, sales had dried up. With no holidays or special occasions going on, I was only getting sporadic corporate orders. To generate cash flow, I decided to try selling some excess inventory on Ebay.

I had one previous Ebay experience before that, and it was not pleasant. I had accidentally purchased two identical books from the same seller. Still, when I contacted him about only buying one book, he threatened to report me to Ebay unless I paid him immediately. I was so freaked out that I paid for both books and vowed to never use Ebay again. However, needing to clear out my extra gift basket supplies, I decided to give Ebay one more chance.

I listed a few items at auction and was shocked at how many

people bid on them! Every day, I would list one or two things, slowly learning how the Ebay system worked, how to deal with customers, and how to ship out items. I was able to quickly liquidate my excess inventory for a nice profit. Next, I cleaned out my personal closet and sold off my old work clothes and accessories. I then began looking for more items to sell on Ebay.

I only had to look at the gift basket wholesalers I was already buying from to find profitable items to sell on their own on Ebay. One of my suppliers not only sold baskets and gift basket making supplies but also stand-alone gifts such as ceramic teapots, plush toys, and holiday décor. On a whim, I ordered some Garfield Christmas ornaments that they had on clearance. I honestly did not think they would sell, so I was stunned when I started them at auction at 99-cents, and the bidding went crazy!

When all the ornaments had sold, and people were still clamoring for more, I was officially hooked on Ebay! By the end of the year, I was done with gift baskets (yup, my gift basket business only lasted one year!) and changed my focus to stand-alone gifts. Annabella's Gift Baskets quickly became Annabella's Gift Shop!

Note: My name is actually not "Annabella," just plain "Ann." When I started my gift basket business, I choose "Annabella" because I thought it sounded elegant. And I have been stuck with it ever since!

For several years, I successfully sold gift items on Ebay. I quickly become an Ebay Power Seller and then a Top-Rated Seller when Ebay added that achievement. After a couple of years on Ebay, Amazon made a very public move to compete directly with Ebay. I was contacted by Amazon and given a few months to try their site for free. Immediately, my Amazon sales overtook my Ebay sales ten to one. While I still sold on Ebay, the vast majority of my sales were now on Amazon. And with Amazon and Ebay pretty much the only online retailers during those years, there wasn't much competition for those of us who sold online. I was able to set the price I wanted, and the customers kept coming.

However, eventually, the rest of the retail community caught up; and Ebay and Amazon were no longer the only online stores. Every major retailer was developing a website to sell their products from. As the online competition grew, even the wholesale companies where I got my products from began to sell online directly to customers. I found myself unable to compete, and my gift business slowly died. I thought my days of selling online were over.

However, my online business was about to find a new life! I had always known that people bought items at garage sales, auctions, and thrift stores to resell. I, myself, had done a little "picking" here and there; but it was never something I took that seriously. After all, why spend hours going from garage sale to garage sale in the hopes of finding things to resell when I could just order brand new items from my suppliers (complete with stock photos, descriptions, and measurements)? With that no longer an option, though, becoming a "picker" (or "reseller," as I prefer to be called) seemed to be the ticket to saving my business.

While I was still selling my gift items, I started going to garage and estate sales to find other things to resell. I started off slowly: a coffee mug here, a plush toy there. At first, I bought a lot of duds that ended up back in my own garage sale pile. But with time, the hits outweighed the misses; and I actually started to make money reselling secondhand items!

It took me about a year of picking before I finally gave up on the gift business completely to focus solely on pre-owned items. I still miss the ease of selling new products, but I am very thankful that there are other items I can make money on! Selling online allows me to work from home and offers plenty of flexibility.

I am also fortunate to have a "volunteer" assistant: my dad! He loves accompanying me to sales and handles all of the cleaning and shipping of items. Buying items, researching them, taking and editing photos, writing listings, answering customer questions, and processing orders is very time-consuming; so, it is wonderful to have a helper!

As great as Ebay is as an income source, it is a lot of work. Finding items to sell is the easy part; everything must then be cleaned, researched, photographed, measured, listed, stored, and eventually shipped. There are customer questions to answer and shipping supplies to buy. No matter how much or how little you sell on Ebay, doing it well is a JOB, and by 2012, I was definitely feeling burned out.

In order to recharge and save my sanity, I decided that a new project was in order; so, I began writing books, such as the one you are reading now. I also developed another income stream via a YouTube channel so that I didn't have to rely solely on Ebay to make money.

These days, I have three businesses: Ebay, my books (both published under my own name as well as journals, planners, and notebooks published under my Jean Lee Publishing pen name; all of my books are available to purchase on Amazon), and YouTube. Combined, these ventures provide me a full-time income. I no longer look at Ebay as my full-time job, but rather as a very well-paying part-time job, one that earns me a full-time income on its own but with me only needing to work part-time hours. And the great thing is that when I need extra money, I simply ramp up my selling. Sometimes I go all out, buying and listing a lot, and when I need a break, I take some time off to recharge. Ebay allows me the flexibility of not only selling what I want but how and when, too. Of all of my "jobs," Ebay has the greatest income potential; how much I make is completely up to how much work I am willing to put in.

While the actual work of creating Ebay listings can be tedious, the fun of going to estate sales and thrift stores looking for items to resell is what keeps me hooked. I love picking up vintage treasures to sell in my Ebay store, although if I find newer collectibles or clothing that I know will sell, I don't hesitate to pick up those things, too. I find safety in the fact that if I NEED money, I can hit up some garage sales to find items to resell that will bring me some cash fast.

I get so many questions from people wanting to sell on Ebay, whether as a full-fledged business or just as a way to earn a little extra money. The number one question people ask me is, "What items should I sell on Ebay?" There are millions of different products out there that you can resell, but in this book, I am sharing with you a list of 101 items that I have personally purchased secondhand and resold on Ebay. These are not items I have heard someone else talk about or things I've only researched in completed listings. These are my tried-and-true finds, ones I am always on the lookout to buy for resale!

This is not a how-to-get-rich-quick book. There is no magic formula or easy system to make millions on Ebay. You are not going to be able to retire selling any of the items I have listed in this book. However, the following pages are filled with things that are readily available in most areas of the country; and if you purchase them at the right (i.e. low) price, you WILL make money selling them on Ebay.

While we would all like to find an antique for $1 that is worth millions, the reality is that most $1 items sell for $10 to $20 online. But to me, knowing how to turn a one-dollar bill into a twenty is what being a successful Ebay seller is all about.

Remember that selling on Ebay is work! The more work you put into finding quality items, taking good photographs, writing detailed listings, securely packaging orders, and promptly dealing with customer questions, the more successful you will be and the more money you will make. Ebay has cracked down on sellers who consistently receive poor feedback and complaints; so, take the time to do things the RIGHT way!

So, if you are looking for easy-to-find, inexpensive things to pick up at garage sales, estate sales, and thrift stores to resell on Ebay, let's get started!

101 ITEMS TO SELL ON EBAY

(In Alphabetical Order)

#1 ADDING MACHINES

Vintage adding machines are a popular collectible that I stumbled upon a few years ago. These machines are HEAVY, but the shipping weight does not deter collectors from buying them. I have sold these anywhere from $30 to $100, depending on the brand and their condition.

I usually find these machines at estate sales, and I only buy them on the half-off days. Most people pass these up, so they are usually one of the items leftover on the last day of the sale. Since condition and brand cause the selling price to vary wildly, I make sure to pay as little as possible for these. The more keys a machine has, plus the overall condition of the paint and decals, are big factors in how much you will be able to sell it for. A machine with lots of keys, for instance, will bring in more than one with only a basic set of numbers. Likewise, for a model where the original paint and decals are in good shape over one that is faded, chipped, and cracked.

Remington, Olivetti, and Burroughs are three brands to keep an eye out for. Since it can be hard to know if these vintage machines have all of their internal parts, I always list them "as is." Collectors can be super fussy, so it is important to protect yourself against an Ebay buyer filing a case against you claiming the adding machine they bought from you was not in the condition you described it as.

If all the keys are working, I will put that in the listing, although I will add that they may be sticky. The ribbons on these machines are almost always dried up, but that is something collectors understand due to the age of these pieces. You do not have to buy a new ribbon; just list that the machine will likely need a new one. As I said, do not make promises that these machines are in perfect working order, as a collector will likely challenge that.

Because these machines are heavy and bulky, we ship them via USPS Parcel Select or UPS Ground. I list these using calculated shipping so that the buyer pays the postage cost for their location. I have a digital scale to weigh everything I list and ship on Ebay so that I can list with the exact weight. Do not list one of these units with "free shipping" unless you have added in the cost to ship them (which is usually $30 or more) into the selling price, or you will find yourself out of money.

Shipping adding machines is where the real work is, but the profit on them can pay off nicely. We wrap the machine in bubble wrap and use a lot of packing material and/or packing peanuts around it to ensure it arrives safely. I always make sure I have a shipping box for these before I list them so that we are ready to ship once they sell.

Adding machines are heavy, but if you have the strength to carry them, can find them cheap and in good condition, definitely pick them to sell on Ebay for a nice profit!

#2 ASICS GEL SNEAKERS:

I have my own pair of Asics gel sneakers, so I know how expensive these are, which is why they command a high price even secondhand on Ebay. I have sold a used pair of Asics gel shoes on Ebay for $65 that I had purchased at a garage sale for only $1!

If you spot a pair of Asics brand shoes and are thinking about buying them to resell, be sure you are getting the GEL version, not one of the standard styles. The Gel shoes are labeled as such, usually on the heel. As with all clothing items, you want to make sure the shoes are CLEAN and in good condition. Check the tread and give them a cleaning with a damp cloth. Take photos from all sides, including the bottoms of the shoes.

Fun colors and larger sizes will sell more quickly than plain styles in small sizes. However, that is true for most clothing and shoes. Asics is always releasing new models of these shoes, making older styles highly sought after by people who do not like the new releases and are searching to replace a worn-out favorite pair.

You can get free Priority Mail shoe boxes from the Post Office, which are perfect for shipping shoes. We wrap the shoes in bubble wrap and then use packing paper to protect them inside the box. Shoes are heavy, so either choose calculated shipping, so the buyer pays the shipping cost to their location, or build in the cost of shipping to your selling price. Smaller pairs of shoes may fit in a Priority Mail Flat Rate Box; so, check that price to see if it comes out less than shipping regular Priority.

There are a lot of high-priced sneakers out there to resell on Ebay, and Asics Gel is just one style to keep an eye out for!

#3 BABY & KID'S GAP CLOTHING:

I f you have ever been to a garage sale, you know that there is an abundance of gently used children's clothing available. There are so many different brands out there, but one I am always on the lookout for is Gap, specifically Baby Gap and Kid's Gap. Gap charges a crazy amount of money for new children's clothing; so, picking up shirts, pants, dresses, and coats for less than $1 at a garage sale will almost always result in a nice profit on Ebay.

If you stumble upon a bunch of pieces of Gap clothing in the same size, even better as you can lot them together. Moms love the convenience of buying a big box of clothing in one transaction. Also, anything that is denim is usually an easy sell. I frequently find Gap Kid's denim jackets for under $2 at Goodwill that I can quickly sell for $20 on Ebay.

Since babies and children tend to make messes, it is important to look over the clothing for any stains or rips. Stained children's clothing does NOT sell on Ebay, so pass up any pieces that are damaged. The more detailed and colorful the garment, the more it will sell for. For instance, you will make more money on a gorgeous little girl's Gap dress than you will on a plain white Gap tee shirt. In fact, unless you are selling it in a lot with several other pieces of clothing, I would not even pick up a plain Gap shirt.

The great thing about kid's clothing is that it is small, making it easy to photograph, store, and ship. I take a photo of the front and back of the piece, along with an up-close shot of the collar and tag area. I also make sure to fill out all the item specific fields of the Ebay listing (and there are a lot of fields available to fill out in the clothing categories) so that buyers know exactly what they are getting. Including the measurements (pit-to-pit, sleeve, and length for tops; inseam and waist for pants) will cut help down on customer questions and returns.

Since clothing is such a crowded category, I usually offer "free" shipping on clothes. However, there is no such thing as "free" shipping as someone, either the seller or the buyer will have to pay for it. If I am going to offer "free" shipping on an item, I figure out ahead of time what the cost will be and build that into the price of an item. If I feel a children's jacket, for instance, is worth $19.99 and can ship via First Class Mail, I will price it at $24.99 with free shipping. That way, I will end up getting my $20 price with enough money left over to easily cover the shipping cost.

Since clothes are not breakable, you do not have to use too much packing material to ship them. We wrap each piece of clothing in a sheet of packing paper before putting it into the shipping envelope, which just gives it an added layer of protection. Whenever you go to package an Ebay order, ask yourself how you would want to receive it if you were the buyer. Following the Golden Rule of doing unto others as we would have them do unto us is the best way we have found to run a successful Ebay business.

Even if you don't have kids, be on the lookout for Gap children's clothing for a quick and easy Ebay sale!

#4 BEADS & JEWELRY MAKING SUPPLIES:

B eading is a popular but rather expensive hobby, so naturally, the beads and jewelry making supplies are great sellers on Ebay. Whether people are selling off their extras or getting out of the craft altogether, keep your eyes open for these hot selling items, specifically at garage sales, where you can often buy them up in lots.

What I love about beads and beading supplies is how easy they are to list. You can put all of the beads together in one bag and take one photo. Or, if you have multiple bags and supplies, lay everything out and take a few photos so that buyers can see each pile up close. Crafters love to sort through supplies, so you do not have to list every type of bead you are selling. When it comes to selling beads, lots are the way to go!

I always include the total weight of the beads, such as "5 pounds of beads", as quantity is important to buyers. Being able to fill up a Flat Rate Priority Mail Bubble Mailer is always a great way to sell beads, too. This also allows you to know the shipping cost beforehand and offer "free" shipping by adding in the shipping cost to the price of the item.

Be aware, however, that not all beads are good for resale on Ebay. Quality is important, so skip the cheap plastic beads that look like they were made for children. Plastic beads are easy to spot as you will see the seam on them. Czech and crystal beads are the ones you want to look for.

Beading supplies such as wire, thread, and tools are also good to pick up if you can get them cheap. As with the beads themselves, putting together lots of supplies is the best way to sell these. To educate yourself about beads, take a stroll through a craft store such as Michael's or Hobby Lobby. You will quickly get a sense of what beads and beading supplies cost at retail.

#5 BETTY CROCKER COOKBOOKS

U sed cookbooks are a dime a dozen, but one brand I will always pick up are vintage Betty Crocker cookbooks. While I avoid the newer titles and the microwave versions, I love finding the old binder and bound hardcover editions that have dust jackets.

I have picked up many Betty Crocker cookbooks over the years, usually paying only $1 for them at estate sales and then selling them on Ebay for $20 or more. Finding a first edition Betty Crocker cookbook will net you an even larger amount, but later editions will still sell well.

One popular Betty Crocker cookbook that is fairly common to find secondhand is referred to as the "pie chart" cover, as the cover features a circle with various recipes pictured in a pie-slice design. In excellent condition, this cookbook is an easy $25 on Ebay.

The older 3-ring binder style Betty Crocker cookbooks are particularly desirable, but they are hard to find in good condition. However, I have sold ones that were falling apart at the seams and missing pages. Check the first pages for a date and edition. The older the date, the better, as these books have been reissued many times over the years.

The binder style cookbooks come with multiple pages and dividers. Often times, some of these pages and dividers are missing. Therefore, be careful when describing the condition of these books. You do not want to advertise a book as complete unless you are 100% sure that it is.

Cookbooks can ship via Media Mail in a bubble poly mailing envelope or in a plain cardboard box. While Media Mail does take much longer to reach its destination, many customers prefer it as it keeps the shipping costs on heavy books extremely low. While you do not have to wrap up books the same way you would wrap ceramics for shipment, you still want to surround the book with packing paper to protect it during its journey.

#6 BIBLES

I learned about Bibles from a fellow picker, and they were one of the first items I started buying to resell. There may only be one Bible, but there are hundreds of thousands, if not millions of versions of the Good Book out there.

In my experience, the older the Bible is, the better it will sell. Also, the more features it has – red-letter, color illustrations, zippered cover – the more valuable it tends to be. I avoid picking up paperback Bibles, which are newer and far less desirable. And I also do not buy books about Bibles, such as books that explain the stories of the Bible in textbook or novel format. When buying Bibles to resell, only buy actual Bibles.

When listing vintage Bibles on Ebay, I usually list the "Antiquarian & Collectible" subcategory, as opposed to the non-fiction section. In the item description field, I include all of the information on the inside cover page, as well as the date of publication. Many old Bible covers are made of hard bonded leather, although some look like leather but actually aren't. Unless a Bible is clearly stamped as "leather," I make sure to list it as "faux" or "leather-like."

On average, I sell most Bibles for $19.99 with free Media Mail Shipping. However, some have only gone for $10 while others have gone for nearly $70. When in doubt of what I should charge, I try my luck by starting the Bible at auction for $9.99. My most recent big Bible sale came from a $9.99 auction when two bidders drove the price of a vintage Bible printed in England up to $66! And they paid the shipping cost on top of that.

Bibles can ship via Media Mail, although some are light enough to go First Class. If a book is 16 ounces or under, I will always choose First Class over Media as the package will arrive much fast (3-5 days versus up to 4 weeks). For the Bible that sold for $66, I shipped it in a Flat Rate Bubble Mailer with plenty of wrapping paper around it to protect it during shipping. For older, very fragile Bibles, you want to make sure the book is protected during shipping, so the spine is not further damaged, resulting in torn pages. Putting the book into a plastic bag and then wrapping it with a sheet of bubble wrap is an easy way to do this.

#7 BLANK CASSETTE TAPES

Not everyone has moved on to MP3 players; there are still people who use cassette tapes, and they search Ebay looking for brand new blank ones. When it comes to blank cassette tapes, the longer the recording length and the higher the quality, the better. Some blank tapes will sell for $5 each, while others may only be worth $1.

I only buy brand new and sealed tapes, and I then save them up until I have a large lot of them to resell. My best sale was a lot of seven tapes that I bought at an estate sale for 25-cents each and then sold on Ebay for $40!

Don't just look for full-size tapes; keep an eye out for the mini-cassette tapes, such as the kind reporters used to use in their portable recording machines. And speaking of recording machines, yes, those sell, too! Of course, before buying any electronic, make sure to test it to ensure it is in working condition.

While blank cassette tapes are a form of media, they do NOT qualify for Media Mail. Therefore, you will need to ship these via Parcel Post or Priority. You may want to base the size of your lot on how many tapes you can fit into a Priority Mail Flat Rate box, as this will usually be the lowest cost option. Since a box of tapes is heavy, be careful about offering "free" shipping. If you cannot add in the price of shipping to the cost of the listing, then use Calculated Shipping and have the buyer pay the shipping cost to their location.

To ship tapes, we bundle them together in sheets of bubble wrap. We then use packing paper to protect them inside of the shipping box. While the tapes themselves are not prone to damage, you want to ensure that the plastic cases do not break during transit.

#8 BLANK VHS TAPES

No one uses VHS tapes anymore, right? Wrong! There are still people out there who are using old media for various reasons (like the blank cassette tapes I mentioned earlier), and since most stores do not sell VHS tapes anymore, people come to Ebay to find them.

I often find brand new, still sealed VHS tapes at estate sales for a quarter. I hold on to them until I have a nice pile and then list them together as one lot. As with cassette tapes, the longer the recording time is on the tape and the higher the quality, the better they will sell. Because the selling price of VHS tapes varies widely, I rarely pay more than 25-cents for them.

As with blank cassette tapes, blank VHS tapes cannot be shipped via Media Mail. You will have to ship them Parcel Post or Priority. And because a box of tapes can be heavy, you will need to be careful if you decide to offer "free" shipping for them as the cost could quickly eat up your profits. When it comes to heavy items like this, I usually stick with calculated shipping so that the buyer pays the cost to have the item shipped to their location.

To ship VHS tapes, we bundle them together using bubble wrap and then use packing paper to protect them in the box. While you may not see VHS tapes as fragile, they are largely made of plastic and can crack or break if dropped.

#9 BLOOD PRESSURE MONITORS

I have been to many estate sales at retirement homes, and at nearly all of them, I have found blood pressure monitors. Both manual and electric units sell on Ebay. I will not pay more than $5 for one of these machines; however, as the average selling price on Ebay is around $20.

It is important to test blood pressure machines before buying them to be sure they are in working condition. It is also vital to list all parts that are included; if you are not sure, take several photos and list "as is." I have found many units that were missing accessories that originally came with them, so I am always careful to list the pieces that are included in the one I am selling.

Make sure to inspect the blood pressure cuff, the part that secures around the arm, to ensure it is clean and that the Velcro is intact. While newer units with digital screens are highly sought after, do not overlook the older models with the baumanometers as many people prefer that style over the new versions.

Antique and vintage blood pressure monitors are often times collector's items that can fetch $100 or more. However, these units often contain mercury, which is prohibited from being shipped by the Post Office. As of this writing, only FedEx handles shipments containing mercury.

Because blood pressure monitors often have glass parts, take care when shipping them. We wrap them securely in bubble wrap and use plenty of packing paper to buffer them against the shipping box. Most of these units are relatively lightweight, meaning I often offer Parcel Post but upgrade the buyer to Priority Mail. Not only does Priority arrive faster, but I can use a free Priority Mail box!

#10 BOWL GAME SOUVENIRS

College football bowl games are a big business, but the merchandise released for them is minimal and only available for a short time. Therefore, for die-hard fans, bowl game souvenirs are very sought after. Better yet, if you live near a major NCAA school that frequently plays in bowl games, the souvenirs are very easy to find to resell on Ebay.

I am in Iowa, so I am always on the lookout for anything from one of the University of Iowa's many bowl appearances as they are always hot sellers. The older Rose Bowl memorabilia is the most valuable, but I have sold items from nearly every bowl game the Hawks have ever played in.

I especially love picking up bowl game mugs and glasses that are in good condition with no chips or cracks. The ceramic steins from the Hawk's 1980's Rose Bowl appearances easily sell for $24.99 on Ebay, and I can usually pick them up for $1 at estate sales. I also look for bowl game hats, tee shirts, sweatshirts, bags, and pins. I recently sold a lot of 16 Hawkeye bowl pins from various years for $29.99; I had paid 25-cents for each.

While bowl game souvenirs featuring specific teams are good sellers, I have learned to avoid general merchandise that only promotes the bowl itself. For instance, I recently picked up a vintage Rose Bowl stadium cushion; however, it did not have anything on it about the teams that played in the game. Football fans of specific teams collect bowl merchandise; there are not really collectors for just general bowl game items.

Ebay provides an NCAA subcategory under the "Sports Mem Cards & Fan Shop" category, and you can then choose the team and bowl game specifics within the listing to help collectors easily find your item.

#11 BOY SCOUT MEMORABILIA

D id you know that people collect Boy Scout memorabilia? Vintage Boy Scout patches, mugs, and other items can command a nice price on Ebay. Special, hard-to-find patches may even start a bidding war.

When I come across Boy Scout patches, I research each one to see if it will sell on its own. If I find that it alone is not bringing in a high price on Ebay, I save it back until I find more so that I can create a lot. Not only are lots of patches easier to list and ship, but bundling several pieces together allows me to charge more as collectors like to get a package of different patches that they can sort through.

If you find a Boy Scout shirt with the patches still attached, those sell, too, although you can cut the stitching and remove the patches if you want to. Be careful when cutting the patches off so that you do not damage the patch itself. Shirts are usually very lightweight, so if you have a shirt with lots of patches, save yourself the time of removing them and just sell the shirt as-is with the patches attached.

If you are at a garage sale or thrift store and you find patches priced individually, be careful not to overpay. While there are some valuable patches out there, many do not bring much money on their own. I try to stick to buying patches in lots unless I am for sure that a single patch will result in a huge profit. I rarely pay more than 50-cents for an individual patch, and I prefer to only pay 25-cents.

The great thing about selling patches of any kind is that they are easy to ship. They can fit in a padded mailer and, as long as the total weight of the package is 16 ounces or less, they can ship via First Class for a few dollars, which allows you to offer "free" shipping as you can easily add in the shipping cost to the price. If you have a large number of patches that weigh over one pound, see if they will all fit into a Flat Rate Priority Mail Bubble Mailer, which you can ship for under $9.

I like to put small items such as patches into plastic baggies and then wrap them in a piece of packing paper before putting them into the shipping envelope. This offers more protection than just tossing the patches into the package, but it does not add much weight.

#12 CARE BEARS

F inding an original plush Care Bear from the early '80s in good, clean condition can be hard, but if you do stumble across one for a dollar or two, snatch it up as they average $20 on Ebay. Be sure to check the tag for a date as these continue to be released in today's market. The ones that sell well on Ebay are dated around the early 1980s.

Cleanliness is important for dolls and plush toys, although most Care Bears can be spot cleaned. If a bear is really dirty, you can try putting it in the washing machine. While these usually clean up well, if they are in really bad shape, they may fall apart in the wash. Hence, I do not buy Care Bears in poor condition.

Do not limit your search just for the plush Care Bears, though; keep an eye out for any vintage Care Bear products such as bedding, books, and other toys. While the stuffed animals are the most common collectible, there are collectors who are after anything Care Bear. Again, look for a date before you purchase anything to resell on Ebay as Care Bears continue to be produced today. I only buy items to resell on Ebay if they are dated from the early 1990s or earlier, with 1980's tags being most desirable.

Plush toys are easy to list, as you just need to snap a few photos; one of the fronts, one of the backs, and one of the faces. Make sure to take a picture of the tag, too. When it is time to ship stuffed animals, first try a Priority Mail box, as often Priority Mail is cheaper than Parcel Select, especially if you are printing your labels from home directly off Ebay. The shipping discounts provided by Ebay almost always make shipping Priority less than Parcel for items weighing less than four pounds. Tall and narrow toys like Care Bears usually fit perfectly into a Priority Mail Shoe Box (yes, you can ship items other than shoes in the shoe-size box).

We lightly wrap plush toys in a sheet of packing paper with a small amount of scrunched up packing paper or packing peanuts around it in the shipping box. Because plush will not break, there is no need to go overboard with the packing materials; but you still want to offer the item a bit of protection from the outer box.

#16 CHARACTER BEDDING

Parents love to design their kid's bedrooms around cartoons, so licensed character bedding is sought after but usually expensive to buy new. Finding these sets secondhand in good condition can be a challenge as the patterns tend to fade due to washing, but if you do find a nice set for a reasonable price, snatch it up. Be sure to check for stains and rips. You want any bedding you pick up to sell on Ebay to be in good, clean condition.

I have sold a Winnie the Pooh baby crib bedding set for $50 that I paid $10 for at a garage sale. I have also sold individual sheets with characters from Disney and Peanuts on them for $15 each. I find sheets and pillowcases all the time at estate sale for less than $1. You do not need to find complete sheet sets or sets with the bedspread or comforter. Single sheets, comforters, pillowcases, and throw pillows sell just fine on their own

Do not just look for modern prints and characters; however, as vintage character bedding also sells well. Often people who are buying vintage sheets are not going to use them for bedding but for sewing projects. So, if you find a vintage Peanuts or Smurfs sheet with a small stain near the corner, you may consider picking it up as a buyer may still want the good section of the fabric.

The biggest issue I often find with bedding is piling, those little furry fabric balls that are all overdue to multiple washes. A tip to remove piling is to run a disposable razor over the fabric, being careful not to cut the fabric or stitching. It takes a bit of time, but the razor does take off all the little furballs.

When listing bedding on Ebay, be sure to disclose whether it is a twin or full size. To take pictures of sheets, spread them out over your own bed and then crop the photo so that any parts of your own bedding or bedroom are not showing. Take a close photo of the print, too.

A big bonus with bedding is that it is easy to ship as you do not have to worry about it breaking. We do put a protective piece of packing paper around the item and then use a bit more paper in the box. But because sheets cannot break, we do not go overboard with the packing materials. We just use enough so that the buyer does not open the box to find their item just sitting there completely unprotected.

#14 CHILDREN'S HALLOWEEN COSTUMES

I am always on the lookout for children's Halloween costumes in GOOD condition. Finding them without rips or missing accessories can be tough, as many are cheaply made and get destroyed after one use. However, I have always had good luck selling the plush baby costumes (such as a bumblebee or ladybug). I can usually pick these up for $1 at garage sales and sell them for anywhere from $10-20, depending on the size and the character. As an example, a Winnie the Pooh plush costume will sell for more than just a general bear outfit.

I am also always on the lookout for Disney Princess costumes and dresses, as they are hot sellers year-round. When parents take their kids to a Disney theme park, they often like to dress their little girls up as princesses. The dresses are outrageously priced in the parks, so moms and dads are always looking on Ebay to find them cheaper.

I always hit up the Halloween clearance sales at Target and Walmart to grab as many brand-new Disney Princess costumes that I can find. Since most come with a big pre-printed price right on the package, I usually list them for that price and with free shipping. Most kid's costumes are lightweight and can be shipped for First Class in a poly mailer, so the few dollars it costs to ship them does not eat too badly into my profits. However, because I am going by the price on the label and offering free shipping, I only pick up costumes when they are at least 80% off, preferably 90%.

When it comes to costumes, I find that the girls' outfits far outsell the boys. Not only are parents buying these costumes for Halloween but also for every day dress up. And girls tend to be the ones with a dress-up wardrobe.

In addition to costumes, I will also pick up the plush Halloween candy baskets. Not the plastic ones, but the ones that look like an actual stuffed animal. I stock up on these when they are 90% off at Target after Halloween, and I have had good luck selling them year-round for the price on the label. Parents buy these for Easter baskets, too, so they do sell well in the spring. Because of their size and their low mark up, I do not offer free shipping on the baskets.

#15 CHINA

There are sellers on Ebay who specialize in replacement china, and if you have the room to store sets of dishes, you can make money –albeit rather slowly – by selling the items piece by piece. While I have sold sets in the past, shipping is a real pain; we have shipped sets of dishes and used more packing material than the items were worth!

However, I do always check out the china at estate sales. Even though the sets are usually priced rather high, I like to look at the individual pieces that are for sale on their own to see if there are any good brands. Fine china will be marked on the bottom with the brand name and country of origin, so it is easy to pick out the good stuff from the generic brands. Since price varies widely by brand and style, I never pay more than $1 for a piece of china unless I am for sure of its value and know that I can sell it for a high price on Ebay.

Note that when I talk about "china," that I am referencing the material (ceramic, porcelain, bone china), not "Made in China." In general, you want to avoid pieces marked "Made in China" unless they are from a good brand. If the only mark on a piece is "Made in China," put it down and move on as it is just a cheap item from the dollar store or Walmart.

While teacups, mugs, and serving bowls may not bring in a huge profit, they can be nice items to have to draw traffic to your other listings. Lefton and Fenton are two brands I look for, as well as pieces that are marked as made in the United States or any European country. British pieces (marked as Britain or the United Kingdom) are almost always good pickups for resale on Ebay.

You obviously need to take great care when shipping china. We carefully wrap pieces in a few layers of bubble wrap and then use plenty of packing material to cushion them in the box. Boxes get tossed around and dropped a lot during shipment, so you want to do everything you can to prevent breakage. Most pieces of china fit in the free Priority Mail boxes you can get from the Post Office, and with the shipping discount, Ebay offers when you ship on their site, Priority Mail often comes out less than Parcel. I list pieces of China using Calculated Shipping so that the customer pays the postage cost to have the item delivered to their area.

#16 CLOCK RADIOS

Vintage clock radios from General Electric (GE) are an item I see everywhere, from Goodwill to estate sales. With clock radios, it is really all about the look of the piece, with Mid-Century Modern or Art Deco lines with traditional clock faces or the flip numbers being the most desirable.

Remember that you are looking for vintage clock radios, not today's styles with digital clocks (unless it has a CD or iPhone charger, which are features that are more important than the clock alone). You can walk into any Target or Walmart store and buy a clock radio for under $10, so be sure you are buying something that is authentically vintage.

How do you know if a piece is vintage? The vintage style radios usually have a wood looking shell or a hard-plastic casing and will have a traditional clock with hands or a flip-style display. Look on the bottom of the piece to find the "Made In" mark. If it says, "Made in China," put it down and move on (unless, as I said, it is a modern piece that works with an MP3 player). If it says "Made in the U.S.A.," it is usually a vintage unit.

One of the most desirable and easy-to-find vintage clocks is the Panasonic RC 5016, which is a flip number style clock set in a faux wood shell. This model was featured in the "Back to the Future" movie and can bring upwards of $140 in excellent condition. Note that while many sellers put the movie title in their listing header, this is keyword spamming and is against Ebay policy. Trust me, collectors know what they are searching for and will find your listing with just the Panasonic RC 5016; there is no reason to risk your listing being flagged by putting the movie name in your title.

Even a clock radio unit that no longer works may still have value as you can resell it for parts. However, finding one of these in good, working condition is best; so, look for an outlet to test it before buying it. Since the price these pieces command can vary widely, I never pay more than a dollar or two for them unless I am absolutely sure of their value.

Take care when packing vintage clock radios as the cases are fragile and can break during shipment. Wrap them in a few layers of bubble wrap and use plenty of packing paper to ensure they do not bounce around inside the box during shipment. As they are heavier items, I list these using Calculated Shipping so that the buyer pays the postage cost to have it delivered to their area.

#17 CLOTHTIQUE SANTAS

Christmas décor, especially Santa figurines, are a common site at thrift stores and estate sales. Many are common "Made in China" dollar store and big box store junk that have no resale value on Ebay. But there are some Santa Claus figures to keep an eye out for.

Recently I was at an auction and picked up a large Clothtique brand Santa Claus figure for $1. He was over a foot tall and had a separate wood base. I wasn't sure if he had value, but for $1, I took a chance. I am so glad I did because he quickly sold for $24.99! I wish I had known the value of Clothtique as I would have picked up a lot more of the figures at that auction.

I often get asked if I only list Christmas items on Ebay around the holidays, but I list Christmas merchandise year-round. Collectors are always looking for pieces to add to their collections, so it is not uncommon to sell Christmas items in the middle of summer.

As with any collectible, the condition of Clothtique Santas is key; and the rarer and more elaborate the piece, the more money it will bring. These figurines tend to be large but overall lightweight, which is nice for keeping shipping charges low. However, their size usually means they do not fit into the Priority Mail boxes, meaning you will need to have another box on hand for shipping.

I do not list anything on Ebay until I know what it will be shipped so that I do not have to scramble for a box when it sells. However, I still check to see if Priority Mail is less than Parcel Select; if it is, we will put it into a cardboard box and put Priority Mail stickers on it. The buyer will have their Santa in 2-3 days, which will result in great feedback.

When shipping, you want to make sure to protect the Santa with bubble wrap and packing paper or packing peanuts. If there is a base, wrap it up separately so that it does not bounce around during transit.

#18 CONCERT TEE SHIRTS

If you have ever been to a concert, you know how outrageously priced the tee shirts are. While vintage shirts can command big money, even a top from one of today's hot artists will usually sell quickly on Ebay. My Goodwill sells tee shirts for as low as $1, so I always give that section a quick look to see if there are any concert shirts. Since tees are so cheap to pick up, even if they only sell for $10, I still make a nice profit.

For shirts from newer, big-name artists, the condition is key. Many singers and bands now sell their merchandise online, so if you are buying to resell on Ebay, make sure the top is in excellent, like-new condition, and don't pay more than a dollar for it as you will likely only be able to sell it for $10.

Vintage tee shirts, as well as bands with a small cult following, however, are another story. To determine whether a shirt is vintage, simply look at the tag. "Made in China" is a clear single that the shirt is newer. However, if the tag reads "Made in the U.S.A.," it is likely to be vintage. While the condition is still important, buyers give some leeway to older shirts as they understand they have been around awhile. A true vintage tee shirt from a desirable artist can fetch $50 to $100 on Ebay!

Tee shirts are very easy to list; I take a photo of the front, the back, and the collar/tag area. I include the fabric and the size, as well as the condition. While I provide measurements for other clothing, I rarely do for tee shirts. I list concert tees in the Entertainment Memorabilia category on Ebay.

Clothes are one of the easiest items to ship as they can be shipped in a poly mailer. We do wrap everything we ship, including tee shirts, in a sheet of packing paper before placing it in an envelope to give it an added layer of protection during shipment. Most tee shirts weigh under 16 ounces, meaning you can ship them via First Class Mail and add those few dollars into the asking price to list them with "free" shipping.

#19 CORDUROY JACKETS

Denim jackets are my favorite coats to resell, but a close second on my list is corduroy jackets. My Goodwill stores often put corduroy jackets in both the coat section and in the women's blazer section, so I make sure to always check both areas. Often these come in fun colors such as pink and red; colorful styles are almost always fast sellers on Ebay

When it comes to corduroy jackets to sell on Ebay, I look for brand names such as Gap, Coldwater Creek, and Talbots, although larger sizes from stores such as Old Navy will also sell. A larger size corduroy jacket usually sells for $24.99 on Ebay, or I will list it for $29.99 with "free" shipping and ship it in a Flat Rate Priority Mail Bubble Envelope.

We wash all clothing we pick up before listing it on Ebay to get rid of that "thrift store smell." Ironing the collars and cuffs will also result in the garment looking better in photos. Speaking of photos, I take pictures from the front and back of corduroy jackets, as well as close up shots of the collar, cuffs, and any other special details. I want customers to feel as though they are handling the piece and getting as good of a look at it online as they would in person.

Another tip when listing corduroy jackets is to make sure to examine the label carefully to see if there is any "stretch" to the garment. Sometimes you will see "stretch" right next to the brand name, but other times you may see 1-2% spandex listed alongside the cotton fabric. Spandex gives the coat a bit of stretch, which I have found helps to sell the piece a bit faster.

We wrap corduroy jackets in a sheet of packing paper to protect them during shipment before sliding the piece into a poly or bubble mailer envelope. A tip for getting bulky clothing into a bubble mailer is to first put it into a lightweight poly bag. The polybag then slides easily into the bubble envelope, preventing the fabric from sticking to the little bubbles.

I have found most corduroy jackets to weigh in at the one to two-pound range, although heavier lined coats can weigh as much as four pounds. Make sure you get a weight before listing if you plan to offer "free shipping" so that you will know how much to add to the price for shipping costs.

#20 COWBOY HATS

I am always on the lookout for vintage men's hats, and my favorite style to resell on Ebay is the cowboy hat. I make sure hats are truly vintage by looking at the inside label. Hint: If it says, "Made in China," it is NOT vintage! Most cowboy hats have a plastic-type covering over the inside top to protect the fabric from sweat. A cowboy hat with the brand name printed right on that plastic coating is a sure sign of a good hat to pick up to sell on Ebay.

Stetson is the best brand name out there, but almost any vintage cowboy hat will sell. Depending on the material and condition, these go from $25 to $50, although Stetsons bring more. While having a box can be valuable with a brand like Stetson, most hats will sell just fine on their own without a box. And if you find an empty box cheap, pick it up and list it on Ebay for the customers who DO want a box for their hat.

Condition is important with all clothing, especially hats. Check the hat over for any stains or rips. While slight wear on a Stetson is not going to deter its value by much, a hat that is falling apart is one you will want to skip.

The only difficulty with selling cowboy hats is that they are usually too big to fit into the largest size of the Priority Mail boxes, meaning you will need to have boxes at the ready to ship them in. Often my dad must fashion a box around a hat as it is hard to find a box that fits exactly. This does add extra work and time to the selling process and is why I never list anything on Ebay unless I first have a plan on how I will ship it when it sells.

I do a completed listing search of all items before I list them on Ebay, including hats. I find that I end up pricing most cowboy hats for $24.99 with the buyer paying the shipping cost. I list these using calculated shipping so that the buyer pays the postage specific to their zip code.

#21 CROCS

Lots of people joke that Crocs shoes are ugly, but there are just as many people who love them. Crocs are made of Croslite, which is a trademarked resin that is soft, lightweight, and odor resistant. Crocs come in a wide variety of colors and styles, with sizes ranging from baby to adult. They are easy to wash and rarely wear out.

There are knock-off Crocs everywhere nowadays, but the genuine ones are still the most popular and most expensive. Genuine Crocs are clearly labeled as such, so just look for the Crocs logo to ensure you are buying the real ones. While you may find them in a dirty condition, they are easy to wash. You can put them in the washing machine or the dishwasher, or you can hand wash them, using an old toothbrush to get off the grime.

While plain color Crocs do sell on Ebay, even better Crocs to look for are the character (such as Disney) or sports team branded versions, which go in and out of production. As with all clothing and shoes, larger sizes usually sell better and faster.

Many crocs are unisex, with the men's and women's sizes both displayed on the bottom. However, since there is no unisex shoe category on Ebay, you will have to choose either the boy/men or the girl/women categories when listing them. I take photos of the shoe from all sides as well as a picture of the bottom.

The Post Office makes shipping shoes easy with their Priority Mail Shoe Boxes. Since Crocs are lightweight, they will usually be within the one-to-two-pound range packaged, making Priority a more affordable option over Parcel Select when paying for and printing labels online with Ebay. Since Crocs are not breakable, you only have to use minimal packing materials. However, do use some packing paper to stop them from bouncing around during shipment.

#22 DOG BREED GIFTS

Items with specific dog breeds featured on them, such as mugs, bags, and key chains, are nice filler items for your Ebay store. Some sell very quickly, while others may take longer to move. However, they are usually cheap to pick up, and I love to have some in my Ebay store for animal lovers to browse through.

Be sure to look over these items carefully for any chips or stains, as the condition of these products is key. People who love their dogs want only the very best for them, which includes the memorabilia they purchase for themselves.

On average, I find that mugs and other dog breed novelties sell for around $10, with the buyer paying shipping. So, I never pay more than $1 for anything with a dog on it. While these are not a big profit item, I do like having them as part of my inventory mix.

I have sold many coffee mugs with a picture of a dog on one side and a description of the breed on the back. I also once bought out a gift shop's inventory of dog breed key chains (during their going-out-of-business sale) that sold for $10 with free shipping. And I recently sold a vintage ashtray with a Collie on it for $10.

While dog-themed items might not bring in the big bucks, if you love animals, they are a fun addition to have in your Ebay Store!

#23 DENIM JACKETS

My number one favorite item of clothing to sell on Ebay, and one of my top five items to resell overall, are denim jackets, also called jean jackets. I am always on the lookout for these jackets for men, women, and children. If I only have a short time to spend in a thrift store, I will focus solely on the denim coats, which are super easy to pick out from the racks.

Denim jackets are one category where brand and size are not as important in terms of then selling them on Ebay. With clothing, name brands and larger sizes are usually better sellers; but with denim coats, I have even been able to sell size extra-small Old Navy jackets. Normally I shun small sizes and cheaper brands, but denim jackets are an exception.

I am easily able to find denim jackets at my Goodwill stores. The regular price they are $5.25, but I can get them for as little as a dollar during a sale. I always look them over to ensure they have all their buttons and are free of any stains or rips. Since denim is such a study fabric, I rarely find condition issues.

As with all clothing, you want to make sure to take careful measurements of any denim jacket you list on Ebay. Every brand runs differently in size, so a large from one designer may fit like a small from another. With jackets, I provide three measurements, which I take with the coat laid out on a table: pit-to-pit (running the tape measure from under the arm of one side to the underarm of the other side), sleeve (from the shoulder seam to the cuff; or if there is no shoulder seam, from the collar to the cuff, noting that in the listing), and body length (from the collar to the bottom hem).

I take several pictures of denim jackets for my Ebay listings. I take a picture of the front, a picture of the back, a picture of the collar/tag, and up-close photos of any special buttons or details. Ebay gives you 12 free photos for every listing, so take advantage of that to provide as many pictures as possible. You want customers to feel as though they are looking at a garment just as closely online as they would in a store.

I usually list adult size modern style denim jackets for $29.99 with free shipping (shipping them in a Priority Mail Flat Rate Bubble Mailer), and I list children's jackets for $19.99 with free shipping (again using the Priority Mail Flat Rate Bubble Mailer). Be sure to educate yourself on vintage denim from Lee and Levi's, as these brands command a much higher price. I recently sold a 1970's men's Lee denim jacket for $99.99!

To get denim coats to easily fit into bubble mailers, I first put them into a poly envelope, which then slides right into the bubble mailer. The poly envelope also acts as an extra layer of protection during shipment.

#24 DENIM OVERALLS

Jackets are not the only denim pieces that I buy to resell on Ebay. I always keep an eye out for blue jean overalls, as they are fast sellers. Some of my Goodwill stores mix in the overalls with the drapes, while others put them with the dresses. So, I make sure to have a look all over the store so that I do not miss any.

I have sold overalls with shorts and with long pants, with embroidery and plain, and in all different sizes, including maternity. Overalls are not something you usually see in the department stores, but there are people out there who love them and who are searching Ebay to find them. Gap has produced many overalls over the years, so I come across that brand frequently. But I will pick up almost any pair of overalls regardless of the brand as long as they are in good condition with no stains or rips. I also make sure all of the buttons or snaps are intact before buying them.

To take photos of overalls, I hang them on a nail against a white wall next to a window for natural light. I take photos of the entire front and entire back, and I then take up-close photos of the tag, hems, buttons, and/or snaps. If there is any embroidery, I take a nice photo of the design as well. I provide the pit-to-pit, waist, and inseam measurements.

On average, I list overalls on Ebay for $29.99 with free shipping, mailing them in a Priority Mail Flat Rate Bubble envelope.

However, I always do a completed listing search first just to see if the size, brand, or style that I have is going for more. I have sold Disney embroidered overalls for $40.

#25 DEPARTMENT 56 COLLECTIBLES

When it comes to selling on Ebay, some brands sell better than others. Sometimes a brand sells well overall, but there are certain lines under that brand that do not sell. Enesco is a brand that usually sells well overall on Ebay, but their lines of Precious Moments and Cherished Teddies figures generally do not.

However, if there is one brand of collectible that I have consistently had good luck reselling, it is Department 56. Department 56 is famous for their light-up Christmas village houses, but they produce all manner of figurines for holidays and general home décor. When I am out looking for items to resell, I turn all ceramics over to check for a brand name. And when I see a piece stamped with Department 56, I always buy it (well, as long as the price is right; after all, I am looking to make a profit!).

I will not pay more than $1 for a basic Department 56 piece, but I will pay more for a co-branded item from a licensed brand such as Disney. I once paid $3 for a little Starbucks Christmas village accessory cart and sold it on Ebay for $25.

In addition to looking for licensed Department 56 brands, I also look for the pieces that light up and/or have movement. Some of these items are so rare and sought after that they do not even need to be in working condition to sell on Ebay. I once paid $1 for a Times Square building from 2000. While the building itself lit up, the New Year's Eve ball did not drop. I disclosed the problem in the listing and sold it "as is" at auction for $28.

Department 56 items are almost always sold with boxes, and while having the box allows you to ask for a higher price on Ebay, desirable pieces will still sell without the box. I did not have the box for the Time Square building, and it still sold. Had it been in perfect working order with the box, however, I would have gotten closer to $100 for it.

Department 56 pieces are made from delicate materials such as resin and ceramic, so it is important to take extra care when packaging them for shipment. Make sure to use plenty of bubble wrap and packing paper or peanuts to ensure the item is protected from the shipping box. Having a thick buffer of packing material between the item and the outer box will ensure the piece arrives to the customer intact.

And as I mentioned earlier in this book, Christmas and special occasion pieces do not just sell during the holidays. Even though it is currently August, I just sold a Department 56 Easter piece for $49.99.

#26 DESIGNER FRAGRANCE BAGS

I f you have ever browsed the department store ads in newspapers, you have probably seen the make-up and fragrance gift sets that come with a "free" logo tote bag. Many people discard the bag, but the bag on its own can sell on Ebay if it is from a high-end designer.

I once picked up a thin YSL cloth bag for $1 at a consignment store and sold it on Ebay for $24.99! Even the small little cosmetic bags can sell well if they are from a high-end brand. You can often find these little bags thrown in boxes at sales, so always take a moment to look through them for any designer names. Be careful, however, to look for stains and tears. People buy these to collect and sometimes to show off, so the condition is important.

If you come across a variety of small makeup bags from various brands, you might consider just selling them together as a lot rather than piecing them out individually. This works best for mid-range brands. However, if you find bags from high-end designers such as YSL, Chanel, or Gucci, they will sell well on their own.

Bags, like clothes, are easy to list and ship. To list, I just take photos from the front, back and interior. Since they are so lightweight, I list them with "free shipping," adding the shipping cost into the price. Polybags and bubble mailers are great for shipping bags as they do not add much weight to the total package. For large bags, we wrap them in a sheet of bubble wrap and then put them in a large poly bag, shipping them Priority. Small cosmetic bags can easily be slipped into a bubble mailer and sent via First Class.

As I have mentioned several times now, we like to put at least one sheet of packing paper or bubble wrap around all items, regardless of whether they are breakable or not, to give them an added layer of protection. This also goes a long way towards impressing customers, resulting in great feedback.

#27 DISNEY DVD'S & BLU-RAYS

At nearly every sale I go to, there are DVDs; but most are only worth a couple of bucks at most on Ebay. However, Disney DVD's and, of course, Blu-Rays are a different story. Disney DVD's are almost always an easy $15 sale on Ebay, with the Blu-Ray versions bringing in even more.

The reason used Disney movie DVD's sell for more than regular films is that Disney issues so many different versions of their classic animated movies, and many are only released for a limited time, making them much more in demand on the secondary market. It is not just the classic movies that sell, though; the new films released by Disney and Pixar are also almost always a quick and easy $15 on Ebay. Check the prices for new Disney DVD's at the store, and you will understand why secondhand copies sell well on Ebay!

Whenever buying any DVD to sell on Ebay, you first want to make sure the disk is actually in the case. It is not uncommon for people to put the case out at a garage sale and forget that the disc is actually still in their DVD player. You also want to check for scratches. A scratched DVD, even one from Disney, is not going to sell.

Often times I find that children's DVD cases are a bit dirty and sticky from little finger getting their food (and who knows what else!) all over the case. We always clean the cases with an antibacterial wipe. I take pictures of the front and back of the case, as well as of the disk itself. While Ebay does allow you to use stock photos of media, I prefer showing a picture of the actual item I am selling, so the customer knows exactly what they are buying.

DVD's can ship via Media Mail in a bubble mailer, but often they are under 16 ounces, so I ship them First Class. Usually, First Class is only a few pennies more than Media, but the customer ends up getting their package in 3-5 days as opposed to up to four weeks.

#28 DISNEY PARKS & DISNEY CRUISE LINE MERCHANDISE

Disney has two theme parks in America (Disneyland and Walt Disney World); parks in Paris, Tokyo, and China; a resort in Hawaii; and four ships in their Disney Cruise Line fleet. All of the parks and cruise ships sell specially branded merchandise. While some items are available to purchase directly from Disney online, most can only be found at the physical locations, which makes them highly desirable on Ebay.

If you have ever taken a Disney vacation, you know how many souvenirs they sell. From shirts and mugs to pins and magnets, Disney puts its logo on nearly everything. Some Disney parks and cruise line pieces are faster sales than others (a Disney Cruise Line tote bag I bought for 50-cents sold within one day for $15), while novelties such as dated souvenirs may take a bit longer for the right buyer to come along.

I especially love finding Disney items from the various resorts, as this merchandise tends to change frequently and sometimes disappears altogether. Disney vacationers develop a love for their favorite resorts and are willing to pay up for any branded items from those hotels.

Disney used to label their park merchandise as either Disneyland or Walt Disney World. However, these days both names appear on the labels. This is a good way to gauge the date of an item. If you find a coffee mug stamped with "Walt Disney World" only, you will know it is from several years ago. If it is marked with both "Disneyland" AND "Walt Disney World," it is a newer piece.

Disney's Hollywood Studios theme park in Disney World used to be called Disney MGM Studios; therefore, anything with the old name is highly sought after. Disney also recently removed the Mickey Sorcerer hat from the Studios, so products with the hat are desirable. And it is rumored that within a year or two, the park will be renamed again, so be on the lookout for cheap Studios branded merchandise as it will likely increase in value over the next several years.

I myself love vacationing in Walt Disney World, so Disney items always catch my eye, and I love to resell them. Disney is one of those names that bring a lot of traffic to my listings, so I am okay if Disney branded merchandise sits for a while in my Ebay store as it works to bring customers in to buy my other items. There is an entire category devoted to "Disneyana" under the "Collectibles" section on Ebay, which proves just how popular Disney items are on Ebay!

#29 DOLLHOUSE KITS & FURNITURE

I am a long-time dollhouse and miniature collector, so these items always catch my eye when I am out thrifting. Last year, I loaded up on kits and furniture at an estate sale during their half-off day. After briefly considering keeping them for myself, I decided instead to list them on Ebay. I made an easy $200 on a $25 investment.

It is not just miniature furniture that sells but also the dollhouse making materials such as lighting kits, flooring, and shingles. Beware of picking up full dollhouse kits to sell on Ebay, though, as shipping them can be extremely challenging due to them being very large and heavy!

When buying dollhouse furniture, it is important to look at the condition. These pieces are fragile, and I oftentimes find them broken beyond repair. Shipping these delicate items can be a challenge, too; you will want to use packing peanuts to secure these pieces in the shipping box to ensure they do not move around and break.

In addition to the wood furniture, be on the lookout for vintage plastic dollhouse furniture and accessories. These were popular in the 1950s and 1960s and can do well on Ebay. Just as with wood furniture, though, the condition is key. Some of the plastic pieces have two or more connecting parts (such as an umbrella for a patio table or the legs on a crib), and often one or more parts are missing. If you have a large lot of furniture, you can put the broken pieces in with the rest in order to sell them.

I like to sell dollhouse items in lots as they are easier to list, and I can command a higher price. Because the condition can be difficult to determine on these pieces due to their delicate nature, I list dollhouse furniture "as is," providing many photos for buyers to look at before they commit to a purchase.

#30 ELECTRIC PENCIL SHARPENERS

A nother item that you might be surprised to find sells on Ebay is electric pencil sharpeners. The older models are much more powerful than the ones sold today, and the most sought-after have a sleek mid-century modern design. I look for the Panasonic brand and for units made in Japan. Prices on Ebay starting at $24.99 and go up depending on make, model, and condition.

As with any electronic device, you will want to make sure any unit you purchase is in good working condition; so, find an outlet and test pencil sharpeners out before you buy them. Before I list a pencil sharpener on Ebay, I clean it thoroughly to remove old pencil scraps and dust. I take photos from all sides of the unit, including the bottom.

Since pencil sharpeners are heavy, I list these using calculated shipping so that the buyer pays the shipping cost for their location. I live in Iowa, so a customer in Minnesota might only have to pay $7 to have a pencil sharpener shipped to them, while someone in California may have to pay $13. Using calculated shipping on heavier items protects you from losing money on "free" shipping and is fair to the buyer as they are paying the exact cost to have the item sent to them.

For items under four pounds, I am often able to upgrade orders from Parcel Select to Priority Mail shipping for only a few pennies more (and sometimes even less) and am then able to use one of the free Priority Mail boxes from the Post Office. Pencil sharpeners get wrapped in a few layers of bubble wrap and are then surrounded by packing paper inside of the shipping box to protect them during transit.

#31 ELECTRIC STAPLERS

J ust like vintage pencil sharpeners, older styles of electric staplers are also great sellers on Ebay. High-powered electric staplers – the kind that is stationary with a slot in front to staple your papers together without having to use your hands to punch a lever down – can often be found at estate sales for a dollar or two. It's hard to find staplers today that have as much power as the older versions, which is why there is a demand on Ebay for them.

Swingline is one of the most common and popular brands of electric staplers out there for resale, although Panasonic and Bostitch are two other names to look for, too. Many of these units were made in Japan; you can find the country of the manufacturer on the bottom of the piece. Vintage staplers in good condition usually start at $30 on Ebay and go up depending on make, model, and condition.

Estate sales are the prime picking spot for electric staplers as they have often been buried away in storage for years. As I have mentioned before, when it comes to electronics, you want to be sure they are in working condition before buying them to resell on Ebay; find an outlet to test out any model before you buy it. However, if you can pick them up super cheap (or maybe even get them free if they are broken), you can sell them for parts.

Electric staplers are heavy but usually small enough to fit into a 7x7x6 Priority Mail box, which you can get for free from the Post Office. My dad wraps these up well in bubble wrap and uses plenty of packing paper to ensure the unit does not move around during transit. Because their weight makes the shipping charge vary by location, this is an item that I list using calculated shipping so that the buyer paying the postage cost specific to their zip code.

#32 EMBROIDERY FLOSS

I love going to estate sales of former crafters, especially if I can find a pile of never used embroidery floss. Usually, I can get a box of floss for $5 or less and am able to quickly sell it on eBay for $25. I do not worry about listing every color or brand, either; I just take a single photo of it all in a big pile. I recently sold a lot of 180 skeins (the term for individual rolls of floss) for $37; I paid $2 for the whole bunch.

When purchasing embroidery floss (or any kind of crafting supplies) to sell on Ebay, I stick with items that are new, never used. Embroidery floss comes rolled up with a small taped label around it. I also make sure to only buy floss (or any fabric or thread) from non-smokers as buyers will complain if they open their package and are hit with the smell of smoke. Most non-smokers are extremely sensitive to the smell of smoke. Since I am a non-smoker, I can smell smoke easily and pass up those items.

Depending on how many skeins you have, you may be able to fit a lot of floss into a Priority Flat Rate Bubble Mailer. I like to put all the floss into a zip-lock plastic bag, then put the bag into the envelope for shipment. Embroidery floss is easy to list AND easy to ship, making it a great item to sell on Ebay!

#33 EMMETT KELLY

C lowns may frighten or freak out a lot of people, but there are just as many folks who collect them. Emmett Kelly is one of the most famous clowns in history, so items bearing his likeness (prints, figurines) sell well on Ebay.

Be careful of buying items that LOOK like Emmett Kelly, however, as they are a lot of dollar store knock-offs out there. Always check the bottom of the piece to make sure it is marked as an authentic Emmett Kelly. The last Emmett Kelly piece I sold was a figuring for $24.99; I had paid $1.50 for it at an estate sale.

To list Emmett Kelley figurines on Ebay, I take a photo of all four sides, as well as a picture of the bottom and a picture looking down at the top of the head. I include how tall the piece is, and I price it at Fixed Price based on the results I find doing a completed listing search.

Be sure to check for chips and cracks on any ceramic figurines you buy to resell on Ebay. Some of the Emmett Kelly figurines are quite detailed and delicate, so it can be easy to miss that the piece has damage. Take care when packaging these pieces for shipment. I rarely find these figures with boxes, so my dad makes sure to use lots of bubble wrap and packing peanuts or paper to protect them during transit.

Figurines are another category of items where I use calculated shipping so that the buyer pays the postage cost specific to their location. I give the customer a choice between Parcel Select and

Priority. Almost always, buyers choose Parcel as it shows up as the first option. However, with the shipping discount Ebay offers for printing labels online, Priority often ends up costing less. So, I usually upgrade packages to Priority, meaning I can use a free box, and the buyer gets their order in 2-3 days. Most Emmett Kelly figurines fit perfectly into a 7x7x6 Priority Mail box.

#34 ESPRESSO MACHINES

With so many people addicted to coffee, in-home espresso machines are very popular as people try to save money by making their hot drinks at home. These machines are very expensive new, but they can be found pretty cheap at garage sales and thrift stores as people decide that hitting up Starbucks is easier than brewing their own coffee.

Know your brands before picking up machines for resale. Keurig, Mr. Coffee, and KitchenAid all make quality Espresso machines that sell well on Ebay. There are also models made in Italy that will go for a high price (check for a "made in" mark on the bottom of the machine).

Because espresso machines can be nearly impossible to test at a garage sale or thrift store, and because they are heavy and bulky to ship, be careful not to overpay. I will not spend more than $5 on a unit unless I am 100% sure that it is a high-end brand and that it is in working order.

If a machine does not work, however, you can sell it for parts. Ebay even has a "for parts" subcategory for sellers to list in. I recently sold just one small part from a Mr. Coffee model for $14. The little glass coffee pots are very breakable, and some people are only interested in buying a replacement rather than the whole unit. Piecing these machines out for parts makes shipping a lot easier, too!

If you are shipping out a whole, intact unit, choose a sturdy cardboard box and use a lot of packing material. If a machine is particularly heavy, you may want to consider shipping it via USP Ground, which can cost less than Parcel Post and offers automatic insurance. A tip for shipping via UPS is to pay and print for your label at home and then drop it off at a UPS store. Avoid taking anything to the UPS Store for them to package as the cost is outrageous. You can easily create a shipment from home, paying for and printing out the label, and then taping it to the box. You simply then drop it off at any UPS Store, where they will give you a receipt to confirm that you left it there to be shipped.

#35 FIGURAL COFFEE MUGS

Mugs are a hit or miss item when it comes to selling them on Ebay. While some mugs are hot sellers, others are complete duds. Many new Ebay sellers hear that coffee mugs sell on Ebay and run out to buy every mug they can. The reality is that while certain mugs DO sell on Ebay, most do not. In fact, MOST things, including coffee mugs that you find at garage sales and thrift stores, do NOT sell on Ebay. Being an Ebay seller means learning how to pick out the one sellable item from every 100 that are unsellable. It takes time to build up this skill.

However, when it comes to coffee mugs, figural mugs are almost always a sure bet. Figural means shaped, not your standard smooth-sided mug. Ones that are shaped like cartoon characters or celebrities are highly desirable. I recently sold a Star Trek figural mug for $24.99, and the buyer paid nearly $9 on top of that for the shipping. Disney figural coffee mugs, especially of the secondary characters such as Goofy, Donald Duck, and Pluto, are also very sought after.

As with any mug or cup, be sure to carefully examine figural mugs for chips, cracks, or spoon marks. Spoon marks are the scratches that a spoon makes on the inside of ceramic mugs when they are used to stir the liquid. While some rare mugs will sell with spoon marks, I generally avoid picking up mugs that have them. Also, check for chips. I recently bought a Shrek mug to sell on Ebay but realized its nose had a huge chip in it right before I listed it. Thankfully I had only paid a quarter for it and caught the error before someone bought it.

To list coffee mugs on Ebay, I take pictures of them from all four sides, as well as a photo of the bottom and a photo looking down into the inside. I measure it for height as well as for the width of the mouth (the opening that you drink out of). If a figural mug is particularly large, I will also measure the width.

I list mugs using calculated shipping so that the buyer pays the postage cost for their zip code. Because the cost to ship a two-pound item can be as much as $14 (for example, if the buyer is in Hawaii), trying to build the potential shipping cost into the price of the item would make the cost look ridiculous. Plus, it would greatly overcharge buyers who live close to me.

Almost all coffee mugs fit comfortably inside of the 7x7x6 Priority Mail boxes that you can get for free from the Post Office. Most mugs fall into the one-to-two-pound range when boxed for shipment, meaning I can usually upgrade the customer to Priority from Parcel using my Ebay shipping discount. We wrap mugs in a few sheets of bubble wrap and then surround them with packing paper or peanuts.

#36 FLATWARE

Flatware is one of my favorite items to sell on Ebay. I find flatware at nearly every estate sale I attend. Some of it is just bundled into a plastic silverware tray or in a baggie, while other full sets are in cases. You will usually find everyday flatware loose at sales, while the fancier sets are in the wood boxes (usually from when a married couple registered the set for their wedding). Of course, estate sale companies charge a premium for the sets in the cases; but ironically, sometimes, it is the loose flatware that ends up being more valuable.

Because prices can vary wildly for flatware, I am very careful not to overpay for them. Every set is unique and commands a different price based on age, pattern, number of pieces, and condition. I try not to pay more than $25 for a set that comes in a wood case because while some can sell for over $150, others may bring in much less.

While the silverware sets in fancy boxes are almost always priced high, the loose everyday flatware that is tossed in bags is sometimes as little as $1. I hit up estate sales on their last day when items are half off. Once I went and bought three sets of flatware; two were in wood cases, while the third was in an old plastic divider tray. I paid $25 each for the sets in the cases and $9 for the set in the plastic tray. The $9 set ended up being a rare pattern from Japan that sold for $100 within minutes of me listing it on Ebay!

Flatware is a bit more work than most items you sell on Ebay as you should clean and polish every piece and research the pattern. I use replacements.com and SilverTableWare.com to research flatware. I start with finding the maker's mark on the back of a piece and then go through the online catalogs to find the pattern. Once I know the pattern, I do a completed listing search on Ebay to see what the sets are currently selling for.

You also want to make sure you grade the condition of flatware fairly, noting any pitting, which are tiny holes or dents. Be careful not to overstate the condition, as what may look barely used to you may appear very worn to a collector. I always put in the phrase "normal scratches from wear," which is common to see in flatware listing. I lay all of the pieces out on a white piece of poster board and take multiple up-close pictures of various groupings.

Most flatware pieces are marked with the brand, and some also have the type of material (Stainless or Silver Plate) and the country of manufacturer. Sets are made in many countries, but Japan and the USA indicate they are older and, therefore, usually more valuable for resale on Ebay.

If you are going to sell flatware on Ebay, it is important to educate yourself on the difference between stainless, silver plate, and sterling silver. Sterling silver is the real deal and commands a high price. Do not advertise flatware as silver or sterling unless you are 100% sure that it is. These days there are lots of people hitting up the garage sales and thrift stores actively looking for silver, so the chances of you stumbling upon any at well-attended sales will be rare. Most estate sale companies know silver and will mark it as such.

Note that you do not have to have a complete set in order for flatware to sell. Flatware was (and still is) a popular wedding gift. Couples would register for patterns, and guests would give them a few pieces. It is natural to find sets with 16 spoons but only eight forks. Many sets also have serving pieces such as butter knives and jelly spoons. Make sure to include the total number of pieces in the listing as well as a breakdown of how many pieces of each style are included (example: 16 teaspoons, eight soup spoons, eight knives, one butter knife, etc.).

If you purchase a set that comes in a box, list it with the box but let customers know that you are willing to ship without the box. Lots of crafters are looking for silverware that they can bend to make jewelry pieces, which is why the more ornate handles bring in the most money. They have no interest in paying the shipping charge for a heavy box. And boxes can sell on their own, especially if they are branded with a maker.

In addition to flatware sets, I also pick up any miscellaneous flatware that I find. A spoon here, a few forks there. I put them into a Priority Mail Flat Rate Box and list them as scrap. Collectors and crafters both like to dig through these lots. I am usually able to sell a box of scrap for $99.99 with free shipping, which is around $14 for Flat Rate.

#37 FLANNEL MEN'S SHIRTS

I f you have ever found yourself facing racks of clothes at a thrift store and felt overwhelmed, I can totally relate! I usually gravitate towards men's clothing simply because there is less of it to go through. While there are 50 racks of women's clothes, there are usually only a few for the men. Laziness often overtakes me at the thrift stores, and I just want to go through the smallest piles. But even then, there are still so many shirts to sort through, which is why looking specifically for flannel shirts is a good time-saving, money-making strategy when sourcing clothes to sell on Ebay.

True flannel shirts – the thick, super soft, fuzzy, cotton kind – are one of the most sought-after pieces of men's clothing on Ebay. You would think they would be a dime a dozen, but the well-made ones are actually harder to find than you might think. I have sold Land's End, Woolrich, LL Bean, J. Crew, Gap, and even Old Navy flannel men's shirts. My prices have ranged anywhere from $19.99 to $29.99, with vintage Woolrich shirts bringing in nearly $40.

As with all clothing, larger sizes sell best; if I am pressed for time at a thrift store, I stick to looking at the extra-large and larger clothing. It is easy to skim through the racks looking for flannel to pop out. And when I do find a flannel shirt, I make sure to examine it closely for stains, rips, or tears. I also make sure the size and brand labels are intact and that all buttons are attached.

We usually wash all clothing before listing it on Ebay. With some flannel shirts, we may need to do some ironing, especially on the collar and cuffs, so that they lay flat in the photos.

When listing flannel shirts on Ebay, I take anywhere from three to five photos. I have a white wall in my office with a nail where I hang clothes from on a hanger. The wall is by a window, which provides lots of natural light. I take a picture of the whole shirt, a close-up shot of the breast pocket and collar, and then a picture of the back of the shirt. If the shirt has more details, such as additional pockets or patches, I will take pictures of those, too.

Because clothing is such a competitive category on Ebay, I almost always offer "free" shipping, building the price of shipping into the price of the item. Before I list a shirt, I weigh it on my digital scale to see if it is under 16 ounces. If it is, I know I can put it into a polybag and ship it via First Class. If it is over 16 ounces, I usually decide to ship it in a Priority Mail Flat Rate Envelope, which costs about $8.

#38 FRIENDS SCENE IT GAME

I am not big into selling secondhand board games as so many have missing pieces. Plus, their large and bulky shape makes shipping them a pain. However, one that I always keep my eye out for is the "Friends Scene It" game, which sells consistently on Ebay for $20.

If I can find "Friends" Scene It for $1-2, I grab it as it is a quick and easy sale. I do make sure all the pieces are included; fortunately, there are not too many parts, so these games are usually intact. These games have DVD's with them, so be sure to check that the disks are all included and that they are not scratched up.

This game is extremely easy to list on Ebay. I take a photo of the front of the box, the back of the box, and a shot of the box open so that the customer can see all of the pieces. I then only put the title of the game and the condition in the item description field.

Shipping board games is a challenge because of their shape. They rarely fit into a regular box, whether it is a Priority Mail box or a regular cardboard box. And while the Post Office does offer a box specifically to ship board games in, it is not very deep, so thick game boxes rarely fit into it.

We often must craft a special box just to ship board games in, so keep this in mind if you plan to list a game for sale on Ebay.

When dealing with oddly shaped items, it is smart to know how you are going to ship them BEFORE you list them. That way, you are not scrambling for a box when you make a sale. If you order from Amazon frequently, hold on to the boxes your orders come in as they are usually longer and deeper, perfect for shipping board games. However, be sure to reinforce these with extra tape; Amazon boxes are typically a bit flimsy, so you will want to make sure they do not break apart during shipment.

While I offer Parcel Select as the first option on most of my listings, it is almost always cheaper to upgrade orders to Priority Mail shipping. This is because I pay for and print my labels directly from Ebay and PayPal, which gives me a discount for shipping online. Because of the weight of the "Friends" came, I list it using calculated shipping with the buyer paying the postage cost for their zip code.

#39 FURS

While new fur items are typically frowned upon nowadays, vintage furs are highly sought after by people who want the look and feel of fur without the guilt of buying a newly-made piece. There are many fashion collectors who love to add vintage hats and stoles to their wardrobes. Just make sure the item has a tag authenticating that it is truly real fur, not a synthetic knock-off.

I often find furs at estate sales; the problem is, they are usually priced too high, even on the half-off days, for me to make a profit. Also, the condition is often a problem with the furs I find as the backs are worn off, or the tags are missing. I do not buy furs to resell unless they have a tag indicating exactly what they are.

The furs that sell for the most money on Ebay are vintage women's fur coats, but the amount they bring in range wildly depending on the style, size, and designer. Some sell for around $50, while others can go for over $200. Therefore, be careful about overpaying, as fur is almost always priced high at garage and estate sales.

The furs I have sold have been women's hats and stoles. As long as the fur is not from an endangered species or on a country's banned list, you are safe to ship furs worldwide.

To list small furs, I take pictures of them from all sides and put the measurements in the description field. I also copy all of the information printed on the label. Small pieces are usually lightweight enough to ship via First Class, meaning it is easy to build the few dollars of postage into the asking price of the item in order to list it with "free shipping."

Note that Ebay announced in late 2019 that they would be restricting the sale of new furs in the coming year or two, so be sure any furs you pick up to resell are vintage.

#40 GRAPHING CALCULATORS

If you have had to buy back-to-school supplies for high school or college kids, you know how expensive graphing calculators are. That is why there is a huge demand for secondhand ones on Ebay. Different models command different prices, with basic units starting at $9.99 and more sophisticated ones selling for much more.

I have bought a couple of duds in the past with the battery compartments eroded out (Note: Always check the battery compartments of electronics for erosion!), but even the duds can sell if you lot several of them together as people buy them for the parts.

Note the difference between scientific and graphing calculators. Both will sell on Ebay, but scientific calculators are more on the low end of the pricing scale, while a quality graphic calculator can sell for over $100, depending on the brand, number of features, and condition. Texas Instruments (also referred to as "TI") is the most common calculator brand and the one that brings in the most money. Be wary of generic brands that are sold at discount and drugstore stores as they are not going to bring in much, if any, money on Ebay.

As I mentioned, even calculators that don't work will sell on Ebay for parts. If you can find broken units super cheap, go ahead and pick them up and save up until you have a lot of several to sell together for parts. Some of these calculators are solar, making them easy to test. However, some do have batteries, usually the small, expensive ones. If you are selling a lot of electronics on Ebay, it is always a good idea to have a variety of batteries on hand to test products.

Calculators are another easy item to list and to ship on Ebay. I usually just take a photograph of the front and the back of the unit; I then copy the information on the back of the calculator into the description field of the listing. These calculators are almost always under 16 ounces, meaning they can ship in a small bubble mailer at the First-Class postage rate. You can usually add in the few dollars it will cost to ship these into the sale price of the item in order to list it with "free shipping."

#41 HAND-HELD ELECTRONIC GAMES

E ven though many people now have phones that they can play games on, vintage hand-held electronic games are still a popular category on Ebay. I recently picked up a vintage Ben & Jerry's game for $1 that quickly sold on Ebay for $24.99!

Make sure to test all games and describe their condition accurately. However, a very desirable game that does not work still may sell for parts. If you find a lot of handheld games that do not sell for much individually, consider selling them as a lot for a faster, easier sale.

Also, be sure to check the battery compartment of anything electronic, including these games, before purchasing them to make sure they have not eroded due to old batteries being left in them. It is always good to keep a variety of batteries on hand so that you can test electronics before listing them on Ebay. I will always state that the game was tested with fresh batteries but that the batteries are not included. Not only do the batteries add weight to the shipment, but you do not want to be given away expensive batteries.

These games are easy to list quickly. I simply take a photo of the front, of the back, and of the battery compartment. I then type in all of the information printed on the back of the unit (make, model, country of origin) into the item description field.

These handheld games are usually lightweight enough (under 16 ounces) to be mailed via First Class in a bubble mailer. I keep several sizes of bubble mailers on hand, including smaller ones for items such as these games. However, even though the envelope does have bubbles for protecting the game, we still wrap them in a sheet or two of packing paper to provide some extra protection.

#42 HALLMARK ORNAMENTS

Hallmark has released thousands of ornaments over the years under the "Hallmark Keepsake" name, but only some have resale value on Ebay. I have found that the light and motion ornaments are popular, as are the ones from licensed brands such as Disney and Peanuts. However, if they are too recent, say from the past year, or so, they likely will not sell for much as the market is flooded with them.

If I can find Hallmark ornaments really cheap that do not bring much on their own, they are a nice item to lot together on Ebay. Sometimes I just like to have things that drive traffic to my other listings, even I do not make too much on that particular product, and Hallmark is a brand name that many Ebay buyers are searching for. As a rule, I avoid the "gift" ornaments, i.e., the ones that say "Baby's First Christmas" or "Grandmother," as those are often dated and are the least desirable.

Unless you know that an ornament is very rare and valuable, be wary of picking up Hallmark ornaments that do not have their original boxes. Many of the ornaments with light and motion only work when hooked up to a Christmas light string, so if you plan to regularly buy and sell these ornaments, you will want to make sure to have lights to test them. Other ornaments require special, expensive batteries; again, be aware of the potential cost to test these ornaments if you find them without batteries.

My best Hallmark ornament scores were two from the Beauty of Birds series. I picked up both the Black-Capped Chickadee and the Blue Bird for $2 each at an estate sale. The Chickadee sold for $199.99 and the Blue Bird for $59.99!

Ebay has an entire sub-category for Hallmark Ornaments under "Collectibles." While these ornaments are marketed for Christmas, they sell year-round. The bird ornaments I mentioned sold in July. I take pictures of the ornament from all sides as well as the box. Be careful to look the piece over for any scratches or missing parts.

Hallmark ornaments fit perfectly into the 7x7x6 Priority Mail boxes that you can get for free from the Post Office. Because they usually weigh under one pound when packaged for shipment, you can upgrade customers from Parcel to Priority for the same or less money, which will ensure your buyer gets their package in three days or less. If you have smaller plain cardboard boxes on hand, you may even be able to ship these via First Class.

While most ornaments come with a protective shell of plastic or foam inside of their box, do not just throw them into a shipping box unprotected. Be sure to surround the Hallmark box with packing paper or peanuts to protect it from bouncing around during transit.

#43 HARRY POTTER HARDCOVER BOOKS

Popular, bestselling books usually do not have too much resale value on Ebay as they are mass-produced and available for pennies on Amazon. However, in the case of the Harry Potter series, the hardcover books are especially desirable as many people want the entire collection, sometimes only to display on their bookshelves.

While you may not find the entire Harry Potter series at one sale, pick up the single books you do find and save them up until you have them seven. You do not want to pay more than a dollar or two each and note that they must be in excellent condition with little to no wear on the dust jackets. A complete set of Harry Potter hardcover books averages around $55 on Ebay (or $65 with "free" Media Mail shipping).

While the single books sell well when put together as a set, even more desirable are the boxed sets, the books that come in a special case. The limited-edition set in a wood trunk case can fetch up to $200 on Ebay; so, if you spot one of these for a good price, snatch it up.

If you are not having luck finding the entire set of Harry Potter books, you can still sell them on their own, although they do not bring in too much. I am typically able to get $11.99 for an individual Harry Potter book with "free" shipping.

Note that while these books can be shipped via Media Mail, it is always a good idea to check the price difference for shipping them Parcel Select or Priority Mail. Depending on the distance the package is traveling, you may be able to give the buyer a faster shipping service for just a bit more money. Whenever possible, I upgrade orders to a faster shipping time as customers love getting their items quickly. And happy customers equal great feedback!

#44 HAWAIIAN SHIRTS

Hawaiian shirts in large sizes and loud prints are typically good sellers on Ebay. The key is picking up the right brands; while some bring in terrific money, others will not sell at all. Saint Laurent is the gold standard, selling for hundreds of dollars. Reyn Spooner is another hot seller, regularly bringing in $200 or more. There are also Disney Hawaiian shirts that command a high price. And you cannot go wrong picking up anything Tommy Bahama, including Hawaiian shirts.

Hawaiian shirts actually made on the Island are one factor to always look for. If a shirt says "Made in China," put it back on the rack (unless it is a Disney print) as it is not going to sell on Ebay. Vintage Hawaiian shirts sell best, but some more modern releases can still sell well. Note that many shopping-mall brands such as those sold at Kohl's and JCPenney also produce Hawaiian print shirts; you want to avoid these as well.

If you are unsure of the brand, check the fabric. Cotton, rayon, and Hawaiian silk shirts are what Ebay customers want. Double-check that all buttons are intact and that there are no stains or rips. Many Hawaiian shirts can appear to be both for a man and a woman, but the placement of the buttons will tell you which the shirt is for. Buttons on the left side of the shirt are women's; the right side is a men's shirt. If you are still confused, compare it to a button shirt in your own home to see which it is.

We wash all clothing before listing them on Ebay. With shirts, we often must at least iron down the collar so that it lays flat in the photos. If you are going to consistently be buying clothes to resell on Ebay, it is worth it to invest in an iron and ironing board, as well as a hand-held steamer. Sometimes we will be able to just iron a collar and then use the steamer on the body of the shirt.

As with all clothing, be sure to take measurements of the chest and body length. As these are short sleeve tops, you can skip the sleeve measurement. Point out any special details such as extra pockets or wooden buttons. Take pictures of the top from the front and back with an up-close shot of the neck/collar/label.

Since clothing is such a competitive category, I usually offer "free" shipping on shirts, building the shipping cost into the price. I ship shirts in poly bags, so I am easily able to get a weight before listing. Shirts under 16 ounces (with all packing materials and enclosures) can ship via First Class, so I know to add about $5 to the price to cover the shipping charge.

#45 HOCKEY MEMORABILIA

Hockey memorabilia is one item that I grab whenever I see it (as long as it's at a good price, of course)! Perhaps because hockey items are not as mass-produced compared to those of other sports contributes to their value. I was at an estate of a hockey enthusiast where I bought up a big pile of random items such as hats, pins, and stickers. I paid less than $10 for all of it and quickly sold it on Ebay as one big lot for $100!

NHL snapback hats in good condition are a very fast seller on Ebay, although I find that any well-made hockey hat, even the newer fitted styles that you can pick up at the mall, will still sell well. Souvenir hockey pucks, player trading cards, pins, stickers, programs, and jerseys are almost always good pick-ups to resell on Ebay.

Be sure to familiarize yourself with the NHL teams, however, as there are lots of local and state clubs out there. I often find memorabilia from our city's hockey team at estate sales, and those items do not sell well on Ebay. Stick to items marked as "NHL" (National Hockey League) to ensure you will be able to make money on them.

Vintage hockey items, particularly from teams that no longer exist, can command hundreds of dollars on Ebay. And look for hats and jerseys from the Anaheim Mighty Ducks as they were founded by the Walt Disney Company in 1993 (as a tie-in to the film) and later sold and renamed simply the Anaheim Ducks. Finding merchandise with the "Mighty" on it is a major score!

#46 HOLLY HOBBIE

I go to many estate sales where the tables are full of little porcelain figurines as well as boxes full of plush dolls, most of which are worthless in terms of selling on Ebay. However, one brand that has some nice value on the resale market is Holly Hobbie.

The Holly Hobbie brand was sold to American Greetings in the late 1960s, and in 1974, Knickerbocker Toys licensed the ragdolls that many girls in the '70s treasured. The most popular Holly Hobbie dolls produced were the ones with blue floral print dresses. Early dolls were dresses in beige/brown colors. In addition to American Greetings and Knickerbocker Toys, you may also see the brand name Carlton on Holly Hobbie products

I have sold both miniature and larger size Holly Hobbie figurines as well as all sizes of the dolls. As with everything I buy to resell on Ebay, I inspect all Holly Hobbie items closely for any damage. I also check for tags on the dolls (usually found on the back of the dolls) to ensure it is an authentic Holly Hobbie as many are handmade. You definitely want to make sure the tag reads "Holly Hobbie" before picking these dolls up to resell. Figures will also be marked on the bottom with the official Holly Hobbie logo.

I have found that the figurines sell equally well whether or not they come with their original box, and some were likely originally sold without boxes, anyway. The figures are either ceramic or resin; again, be sure to check for cracks or chips.

Package these carefully using bubble wrap and plenty of packing paper or peanuts to protect them during transit.

In addition to figurines and dolls, you may come across other Holly Hobbie branded merchandise such as bedding and décor. I have found that most anything Holly Hobbie is a good pickup if you can get it cheap enough. If you find dinnerware with Holly Hobbie on it, snatch it up as sets can sell for up to $300 on Ebay!

#47 HOME-BASED/ DIRECT SALE MERCHANDISE

Pampered Chef, Thirty-One, and Scentsy are just a few of the dozens of direct sale companies out there with consultants selling their wares at home parties. There are also a lot of people getting OUT of the home party business and selling off their leftover supplies. These items can bring some nice money on Ebay as new or more successful consultants are looking to stock up on supplies at a lower price than they can get from the company directly.

I find these types of direct sale consultant supply items sell better in lots. Years ago, I was a consultant for The Body Shop at Home, which is no longer in existence. When I quit, I sold my supplies off in lots and recouped a large portion of the money I had originally spent on them.

These days, I am a Thirty-One independent sales consultant, so not only can I buy Thirty-One bags and totes at a discount, but I can resell them easily when I want to try a new style!

One direct sales company you want to be wary of picking up to resell is Avon. If you hit up enough garage and estate sales, you will come across vintage Avon perfume bottles. While there are a few models that will sell for a little bit of money, most are completely unsellable on Ebay. However, vintage Avon jewelry is another story; some of the older pieces can bring in hundreds of dollars.

The bottom line when it comes to selling consultant supplies or direct sales products on Ebay is to not overpay. Unless a piece is extremely rare, it usually will not bring in what it originally sold for. And while some products sell pretty easily (clean, like-new Thirty-One bags sell very quickly), other items are hit-and-miss (I have had great luck with certain Pampered Chef items but could not give others away). The supplies consultants use (clipboards, order forms, displays, etc.) are the items you can usually find for the least amount of money that will net you the largest return.

#48 HOT ROLLERS

H air curlers are one of the items that I still cannot believe sell on Ebay, but they do! The older the model, the better as newer units do not heat up as well as the vintage ones. I have sold used hot roller sets for $80, although the ones I usually find are in the $25 range. And I have ended up only getting $10 for some sets.

Because of the wide range of prices these can bring on Ebay; I am very careful not to pay more than a few dollars for hot roller sets unless I am absolutely sure they are a high-value model. Having all of the curlers intact is important, and while having the clips is nice, most models still sell well without them. Be sure to test them out to make sure they work. We also always clean the rollers to make sure our customers aren't getting curlers with old hair stuck in them!

Remington Tight Curls and Lady Schick roller sets are two of the brands that sell for anywhere from $60 to $90, depending on condition. Jibere is another brand to look for as their curlers average about $50 on Ebay.

Hot roller sets are an item that I list using Calculated Shipping so that the buyer pays the shipping cost. These sets can weigh anywhere from 4 to 6 pounds once packaged, so the shipping price can be as much as $15, depending on where the customer lives.

Because these curler sets are plastic, they are susceptible to cracking and breakage during shipment. We put some light packing paper inside around the curlers and then wrap the entire unit in a few sheets of bubble wrap. We then use plenty of packing paper to secure the set in its shipping box.

Hot roller sets are usually an odd shape, meaning you will need a slightly larger box to ship them in. Because of the discount, we receive when buying and printing labels online through Ebay, we usually ship curlers in the larger 12x12x8 Priority Mail box, which we get for free from the Post Office. This usually comes out to be less than Parcel Select after the discount you get when you ship directly through Ebay.

#49 HYMNALS

Along with Bibles, I love to pick up vintage hymnals to resell on Ebay. I find hymnals, which are church songbooks, all the time at estate sales for $1 or less, and sometimes even for free. There are lots of people who collect hymnals, which makes them a relatively easy item to sell on Ebay.

If I find several hymnals of the same denomination (Lutheran, Baptist, etc.), I will often lot them together in one listing on Ebay. On average, I will sell a lot of five hymnals for $29.99 with free Media Mail shipping. However, I also sell plenty of single hymnals on their own, usually for $14.99 with free shipping (First Class for books under 16 ounces, Media Mail for books over 16 ounces). While I can usually make more selling hymnals one by one, it is faster and easier to list and then ship several at once.

Vintage hymnals, like vintage Bibles, are an item that will sell despite being in poor condition. Of course, a very old hymnal in good condition will bring in the most money; but I have sold hymnals from the 1930s with broken spines and missing pages. Because I have never had a hymnal not sell on Ebay, I rarely pass one up unless the seller has it priced too high.

When listing hymnals for sale on Ebay, I take pictures of the front cover, the back cover, and the spine. I then take photos of the first pages where the title, publisher, and date are. Finally, I take two to three photos of the actual song pages.

Just as I do with Bibles, I basically copy the front page of each hymnal into the Ebay item description field. Buyers like to know how many songs a hymnal has, and most books number the songs separate from the page numbers. So, you might have a book with 800 songs but only 300 pages. Measuring the book itself is also a good idea as you would be surprised by how many customers want to know this.

Hymnals are eligible to be shipped via Media Mail, but for books weighing less than 16 ounces, I will ship them via First Class, which is often a bit less than Media at that weight. We normally ship hymnals in bubble mailers, although we do keep some smaller boxes on hand for thicker books that do not fit inside the envelopes.

#50 JCPENNEY AND SEARS CATALOGS

D o you remember flipping through the JCPenney and Sears Christmas catalogs that came out every year? I do, and so do a lot of other people who now want to get their hands on a piece of their childhood. The regular seasonal catalogs also sell as people collect them or want them for the retro photos.

I recently picked up an early 1990's JCPenney catalog that was still shrink-wrapped for $2 and sold it on Ebay for $19.99. Since these catalogs contain outdated advertising, they can ship via Media Mail, which saves on the shipping charges for these heavy books. Because the pages are thin and prone to tear, you want to ship these catalogs in a box, not an envelope, using plenty of packing paper around them to protect them during transit.

Note that condition is important for getting top dollar for these catalogs. People tended to look through these books a lot, meaning it is hard to find them without missing covers or ripped pages. However, because people threw these away when a new catalog came out, there are not that many to be found. So even books with some condition issues can still sell on Ebay.

As I mentioned, the Christmas catalogs are the ones that command the highest prices; and the older the book, the more money you will get. Catalogs from the 1960s and earlier can easily command over $100 on Ebay. Sears produced these catalogs for many more years before JCPenney's, which did not start issuing these until 1963. JCPenney's Christmas catalogs are not as desirable as Sear's, but on average, they still sell for $40 on Ebay.

#51 JOHN DEERE COLLECTIBLES

My dad worked for John Deere for 29 years and was an avid collector of their toy tractors and other branded memorabilia. He filled the basement of his house with toys, hats, and even a replica wooden wagon. John Deere has four plants in the town I live in, so John Deere items are pretty easy to find here. And John Deere products sell very well on Ebay.

I look for vintage John Deere products, identifiable by the leg position of the deer. A deer with his hind leg DOWN touching the ground is the newest logo; so, I look for the deer with his hind leg UP in the air, which signifies a vintage piece. Since I often find so many little John Deere novelty items such as stickers, pens, and pins, I like to sell them together in lots for a faster sale at a higher price than I would get by piecing them out individually.

Vintage snapback hats with a patch of the John Deere logo are particularly hot sellers. The condition of the hat itself does not have to be in great condition if the patch itself is rare. Most collectors display their pieces; they do not actually wear them. So, it is the patch, not the hat, they are after.

John Deere has expanded their logo license in recent years, so there is quite a bit of merchandise out there, some of it even sold at Walmart. While some of these pieces do sell on Ebay if they are no longer available in stores, be careful about overpaying for mass-produced items that can still be purchased at the big box retailers. Most of these new products are marked as "Made in China" and are dated late 2000 till the present time.

Of course, the most famous John Deere toys are the die-cast tractors. These can be very collectible, but people also tend to price them high at sales. They also tend to be in very poor condition after having been played with. Unless you are an experienced collector yourself and know what toys are and are not valuable, do not overpay for these pieces. If you do come across a bunch of these toys that are not in very good shape but are priced low, you still may be able to sell them for parts as there are collectors who restore these toys.

One John Deere item to avoid buying for resale on Ebay is NASCAR branded products. John Deere sponsored a NASCAR racing car driven by Chad Little in the 1990s. While a lot of merchandise was produced and purchased by collectors, they are no longer popular and typically do not sell well on Ebay.

#52 JORDAN ERA CHICAGO BULLS MEMORABILIA

The Chicago Bulls are one of the most popular NBA basketball teams in history, and items from the Michael Jordan era are especially hot! Michael Jordan #23 jerseys sell for upwards of $60 on Ebay, depending on size and condition. Hats and other Bulls memorabilia such as tee shirts and coffee mugs from when Jordan played have always been fast sellers for me, too.

If you live in Illinois or the surrounding states, you will likely have good luck finding Michael Jordan and Bulls items at garage sales and the thrift stores as so many people in the Midwest are fans. Bulls items sell well on their own, but Bulls products WITH Michael Jordan on it will sell even better. I find Bull's coats and jackets all the time at my Goodwill, picking them up for as little as $1.

Along with the jerseys, snapback hats featuring Jordan also sell well on Ebay. An authentic Jordan hat will have a Nike label (unless it is from the 1992 Barcelona Olympic Games, which were sponsored by Reebok). Nike also produces Air Jordan shoes, which continue to be made and are always hot sellers on Ebay.

Be aware, however, that there are a lot of counterfeit Air Jordan sneakers out there; unless you know exactly how to spot the fakes, be careful of buying these to sell on Ebay. If you list of pair of fake Air Jordan's on Ebay, your listing will be pulled as Ebay actively seeks out counterfeit items

#53 KEURIG
COFFEE MAKERS

Have you ever looked at Keurig coffee makers in the stores? They are very popular, but they are also very expensive. They sell used on Ebay for roughly 25% less than new, so they are an item you can pay a bit more for when it comes to buying them for resale.

It is very important to only pick up Keurig machines in working order unless you get a broken one super cheap that you can piece out for parts. Coffee maker parts, including those for Keurig machines, are easy to list and easy to ship; often, you can make more from the parts than you can on a complete unit.

The Keurig coffee pods will also sell on Ebay; I have found brand-new boxes of these at garage sales for $1. Make sure to check the expiration dates, though, as no one wants coffee that expired two years ago. There are also disposable coffee-pod holders that sell well on Ebay, too.

I bought my dad a Keurig for Christmas one year, but he eventually decided he liked his regular coffee maker better. I sold his machine on Ebay for $90, with the buyer paying the shipping. I had paid $125 for it originally, and he had used it for about a year; $90 was a very good return.

The only bad thing about Keurig machines is that they are large and a challenge to ship, so be prepared with a box and shipping materials before you list one so that you are ready when it sells. Because of the weight, you will likely end up shipping these machines out via Parcel Select.

This is the type of big, bulky, heavy item you will want to list using calculated shipping so that the buyer pays the shipping cost to their location. Also, be sure to pack these machines well, even if they come in their original boxes with Styrofoam inserts. Use lots of bubble wrap and packing paper or peanuts to ensure the unit is secure during transit.

#54 LITTLE HOUSE ON THE PRAIRIE BOOKS

I still have my set of "Little House on the Prairie" books from when I was a child. And if you can find a vintage set in either blue or yellow from the 1970s in very good condition (condition is key!), then you can turn a nice profit on Ebay. I recently picked up a set of these books with the blue covers in their original box for $1.50; they sold on Ebay for $23!

Note, though, that condition is everything with these books. Be sure to check for wear to the covers, a loose spine, and missing or torn pages. I pass up many of these sets because of the damage from them being read so many times.

These sets were originally sold in boxes, so finding them with the box is best, although a set of loose books in excellent condition will still sell. These sets originally came with nine books. In later years, more books have been released under the "Little House" name; these can go for even more than the original series as they were not as mass-produced.

While the paperback Little House books are the most common, if you find any of Laura Ingalls Wilder's books in hardcover, snatch them up as these are rare and can fetch $100 or more on Ebay.

Condition is still important in order to get top dollar on the hardcover books, but since the hardcover versions are rarer, they will still sell with some condition issues.

These books are eligible for Media Mail, so these are good items to list with "free" shipping, building the cost of shipping into the price. Before listing, put the books in the box you are likely to ship them in and get a weight. Then check the USPS website to see what Media Mail would cost. I always use a zipcode from the farthest place in the United States it could go, such as Hawaii. Whatever that cost is, I then add it into the price of the books and list it with the "free" shipping.

#55 LONDON FOG TRENCH COATS

If you have ever scoured the racks at your local thrift store, you have probably come across London Fog trench coats. Beige is the most common color and one that I have learned to avoid trying to resell on Ebay (unless they have a fur collar; those are better sellers). The color coats, however, can bring in a very nice profit.

I look for London Fog coats in colors such as green, blue, red, and black, and I make sure they are in good condition with all of the labels intact as well as all buttons. Note that these often have the size labels inside the flap instead of the collar; check both sides of the inside flaps to find all of the labels, which are often sewn in.

Be sure to check to see if the tie belt around the waist is intact; if it is not, be sure to disclose that in the listing. Note if the coat is lined and how many pockets it has. Provide measurements for the chest (running a tape measure from under one armpit to the other), the sleeves (running a tape measure from the shoulder seam to the cuff; if there is no shoulder seam, run the tape measure from the collar to the cuff and note that is how you took the measurement in the listing), and the body length (running the tape measure from the collar to the hem). Take photos of the front, back, collar/tag area, the inside tags, and up-close shots of any special details such as buttons and pockets. Ebay gives you

12 free pictures with every listing, so take advantage of this to provide lots of photos, which will, in turn, help sell your items fast.

London Fog trench coats are very heavy jackets, so I usually list them for between $40-50 with free shipping. I can ship them in a big polybag that weighs practically nothing, so the only shipping weight comes from the coat itself. I go to the USPS website to see what the shipping cost of the jacket would be to Hawaii (which is the most expensive distance from me) and add that cost into the price. Or I check to see if they will fit into one of the Priority Mail Flat Rate boxes and add that $9 into the asking price.

#56 MATCHBOOKS

For years, my dad collected matchbooks. He filled scrapbooks with his collection and also kept some whole in boxes. Most he picked up for free at restaurants and while on vacations, while others he paid pennies for at garage sales. When he finally decided to let go of his collection, I separated them into lots of similar themes and sold them on Ebay. His entire collection sold for over $400!

The problem with finding matchbooks to resell on Ebay is that many people know they are collectible. They are often overpriced at garage sales, and if they are priced low, they are often the first things to sell. So be on alert if you see them, but also be careful not to get excited and overpay for them as you want to leave plenty of room for profit when you list them on Ebay.

While there are certainly matchbooks that will sell individually, I prefer just piling them into lots as they are easier to list and ship. Plus, the buyer has the fun of buying a lot that they only know a little about but can then search through for treasures!

Most collectors prefer whole matchbooks, meaning the matches are still in them. Many collectors, like my dad, pull the matches out and put the cardboard holder on scrapbook pages. However, some collectors do by the scrapbooks full of matchbooks, so do not pass them up if you find them cheap.

Vintage matchbooks from the 1930s through the 1950s,

Hawaiian matchbooks, and matchbooks featuring "girly" pin-ups sell the best. Avoid common, mass-produced matchbooks that are still distributed today.

#57 NCAA SPORTS MEMORABILIA

I have had great luck with NCAA team items, especially from small, private schools. Since many people are loyal to their home or college team but move to a different state as an adult, there are always people on Ebay looking for certain team merchandise.

Here in Iowa, I find a lot of shirts, hats, and coffee mugs from the three big state schools: University of Iowa, Iowa State, and the University of Northern Iowa. However, I also pick up a lot of products from private colleges such as Wartburg. During a Goodwill sale, I am easily able to pick up collegiate hats, coats, jackets, polos, and sweatshirts for as low as $1 each. And most estate sales I attend have mugs, pins, and other memorabilia from not only Iowa colleges but also from schools across the county (as the owners of the homes or their children attended school out-of-state).

While clothing and coffee mugs are understandably going to sell well on Ebay, do not overlook other items that do not have such an obvious appeal. I recently picked up a tote bag from the University of Iowa bagpipers club for 25-cents at an estate sale. It sold within minutes of me listing it for $24.99. I have also sold awards, trophies, and plaques representing different school clubs.

My general rule of thumb is that if a collegiate item is in good, clean condition and priced low, I pick it up to resell on Ebay!

#58 NORMAN ROCKWELL FIGURINES

I once scored some Norman Rockwell figurines at an auction for $1 each, and I was thrilled to find that they sell for upwards of $30 on Ebay. These figures are sturdy pieces, yet most are small enough to fit in a 7x7x6-inch USPS Priority Mail box. The ones I bought did not come with their original boxes, but they still sold well.

However, while I have found Norman Rockwell figurines to sell well on Ebay, I have also learned that other Norman Rockwell items are not worth picking up. Hit up enough garage sales and thrift stores, and you will likely come across ceramic Normal Rockwell coffee mugs; and while very nice looking, these do not sell for much, if at all, on Ebay.

There are also Norman Rockwell Christmas village houses. At the auction where I picked up the figures, I also bought several of these buildings. Unfortunately, like Norman Rockwell coffee mugs, the Christmas village pieces are not worth much on Ebay.

Normal Rockwell pieces are clearly marked on the bottom as such. If you do spot figurines, be sure to look them over for any chips or cracks. These are highly detailed, which makes them susceptible to parts breaking off.

To list these, I take photos of them from all sides, as well as a photo of the bottom. I price them based on the results from the completed listings; I sell these at Fixed Price, not auction. These are not items that will start a bidding war; to ensure top dollar, you will want to set your price so that buyers can purchase them outright.

#59 NOVELTY MEN'S TIES

The Goodwill stores I shop at all have men's necktie sections, and I always give them a quick scan to see if there are any novelty prints. I look for any kind of cartoon character, college, pro sports team, or advertising. I have sold Disney, Looney Tunes, Garfield, Simpsons, and McDonald's ties, along with lots of sports teams and university school ties.

Rush Limbaugh has a line of ties; I once bought one for 50-cents and sold it for $15! Most of these ties will sell for $10 with free shipping, but ones that feature hard-to-find characters can sell for much more. While regular men's ties sell best if they are silk (not polyester), novelty ties sell because of their print, so the fabric is not as important.

Before buying ties to resell on Ebay, make sure to check them over thoroughly for stains. Many men spill on their ties, hence why they end up at the thrift stores. Recently I spotted a gorgeous Mickey Mouse tie at Goodwill; unfortunately, there was a huge stain right on Mickey's face!

Also, check ties over to make sure there are no rips along with seams, as this is another common occurrence. I only buy ties with the labels still intact, not cut off. If the material is washable, we will wash ties before listing them. Often a quick run of the iron is all it takes to get them looking as good as new.

When I list ties on Ebay, I fold them up nicely to take the main photo. I then take an up-close photo of the print along with a photo of the back where the tag is. Ebay provides item-specific fields for ties, including a slot to put in the width (which you measure at the widest part of the tie).

Shipping ties is a breeze as you can just put them into a poly or bubble mailer. Since they are under 16 ounces, they can be shipped via First Class Mail for under $5, with the buyer getting their order in under five days.

#60 NASA MEMORABILIA

I often come across NASA souvenirs at estate sales, memorabilia the owners picked up during summer vacations spent in Florida or Texas. There are hats, shirts, glasses, coffee mugs, buttons, magnets, pens, stamps, medals, patches, and more commemorating the various space centers and flights, and most of them sell on Ebay. The price they bring varies on the rarity and collectability of the piece, of course, but I pick up anything from NASA that is priced low as it usually brings in at least $10.

Vintage NASA collectibles from the spacewalks, Apollo 16, and the Challenger disaster sell better than modern trinkets. Note that the items that bring in the most money are original pieces, not products that are reproduced to commemorate events. I have sold small plaques commemorating spacewalks for $10, but they were created for anniversaries of the events, not during the actual times they occurred.

Souvenirs from the various space centers and flights sell on Ebay, although the price, of course, varies widely between mass-produced items and one-of-a-kind pieces. I have sold some small plaques commemorating spacewalks in the $10 range. There are a lot of NASA buffs out there, so I always keep an eye out for logo merchandise.

Note that autographed photos of famed astronauts can sell for big money on Ebay, but if you spot these at a garage sale or thrift store, be sure they come with a certificate of authenticity. Autographs are one of the most commonly forged items on the resale market; so, if you cannot guarantee an autograph from an astronaut is real, pass it up as it is not going to sell for much on Ebay.

#61 OLYMPICS MEMORABILIA

I am always on the lookout for Olympic souvenirs. Not only am I a big fan of watching the Games, but I have learned that Olympic memorabilia can sell well on Ebay!

Memorabilia from Games held overseas sells best as they are harder to get a hold of here in America. Items from the Los Angeles and Atlanta Games were readily available here during 1984 and 1996, respectively (I remember buying an Atlanta Olympics mug at the local grocery store), so only the really special pieces from those Games will sell well on Ebay.

If you find an Olympic item such as a pin or hat is not selling, consider relisting it when the next Games come around. With the Winter and Summer Games cycling every two years, another two weeks of competition is always around the corner. Interest in Olympic collectibles spikes when the Games are actually going on and televised.

There are lots of Olympic collectibles on the secondary market. Hats, pins, mugs, and plush mascots are the ones I come across the most often. I have had particularly good luck with ceramic steins commemorating a Games; I once picked up a stein from the Atlanta Olympics for $1 at a garage sale that I sold for $24.99 on Ebay.

#62 PANTYHOSE

If you ever spot me at Goodwill, you may just find me over in the underwear section looking through the bins for pantyhose! I am always looking for NEW, higher-end pantyhose brands that are new and still sealed in the package. Jockey, Hanes, and any other brands sold at nicer department stores sell really well in lots of like sizes on Ebay. Usually, I find a bunch in the same size, meaning one person donated them because they no longer fit or were no longer needed.

I am usually able to pick up sealed packages of pantyhose for 50-cents; on average, I sell them for $5. While that does not seem like much, consider that I lot several packages together. So, I may buy ten pairs for $5 and sell them together in a lot for $50.

Particularly desirable for selling on Ebay are vintage pantyhose and pantyhose packages with famous models on them. However, newer ones still bring in good money; and as with all clothing, larger sizes sell faster than smaller ones.

Listing new pantyhose on Ebay is super easy, too, as I just take a picture of the front and back of the package. I then copy the information (brand, size, color) right off the package and put it into the description section. Since pantyhose are lightweight, even when in a lot, and unbreakable, you only need to lightly wrap them in a bubble mailer or small box to ship them.

#63 PEANUTS COLLECTIBLES

While the popularity of some cartoons come and go, the Peanuts have remained extremely collectible ever since I started selling on Ebay. Charlie Brown, Snoopy, and the entire gang are almost always a good pickup.

Not only are you able to find vintage Peanuts collectibles at estate sales and thrift stores, but there are also modern pieces to look out for. Hallmark releases several new Peanuts Christmas ornaments every year (and sometimes also for other holidays such as Easter and Halloween). These are often the first ornaments to sell out in stores, which creates a big demand for them on Ebay.

My favorite Peanuts find was a Fire King mug from the '60s that I bought at Goodwill for 50-cents. It sold on Ebay for nearly $20! I have also sold vintage Peanuts children's bedding and plush toys.

As with most hot collectibles, there are also some cheap versions of Peanuts items that you can currently buy at Walmart. Therefore, before buying any Peanuts item to resell, be sure to look for a mark, usually on the bottom. If there is a recent year along with "Made in China," you may want to skip it unless it is priced very low.

There are many Peanuts collectors who live outside of the United

States, so shipping internationally will definitely help when selling Peanuts items. Fortunately, Ebay now makes shipping to Canada, South America, and overseas extremely easy with their Global Shipping program. When you opt into Ebay's Global Shipping Program, you ship any items sold to international customers to a warehouse in Kentucky, where Ebay takes full responsibility for re-labeling it for shipment. And if the package is lost during transit, Ebay refunds both you and the buyer the full amount of both the selling price and shipping.

I will admit that I was skeptical of Global Shipping when it first came out, but now I cannot imagine living without it. I used to spend so much time filling out customs forms and lost packages, but now Ebay handles all of that for me. Since I pay and print for my labels right on Ebay, the shipping label prints out ready to be sent to Ebay's Global Shipping center, and once it leaves my house, I do not have to worry about it again!

Back to Peanuts: Be sure to look for the registered Peanuts trademark on all items you pick up to resell. I recently bought what I thought was a Snoopy piggy bank at an estate sale. But when I got home and could not find any maker's mark, I realized it was a homemade crafted piece, not an authentic Peanuts collectible.

#64 PEPSI COLLECTIBLES

C oca-Cola was a hot collectible for many years, but it has definitely died down recently. Once you see items popping up at Walmart, you know they have been overly mass-produced. Pepsi-Cola items, however, are much rarer, which is why I always pick up any Pepsi collectibles that I see.

Vintage Pepsi items such as mesh snapback hats with a Pepsi logo patch can sell for $25 or more on Ebay. I have also sold a vintage Pepsi glass for $25. Yes, $25 for ONE glass!

In addition to hats and glasses, be on the lookout for Pepsi shirts, signs, mugs, and pins. Old Pepsi bottles, even empty ones, can bring in hundreds of dollars on Ebay. While vintage items need to be in excellent condition to bring in top dollar, even things that are not perfect will likely still bring in some money.

As I have mentioned before, I live in Iowa and find lots of Iowa Hawkeye bowl game memorabilia. I frequently find both full and empty bowl game Pepsi commemorative bottles. Full bottles from the 1980's Rose Bowl games sell upwards of $25, and I can usually pick them up for a dollar.

There are very few items that I will always pick up, but Pepsi products are one of them!

#65 PERFUMES

Have you ever been to a thrift store or an estate sale and come across a dusty old perfume bottle that was half empty? You probably thought it was junk, but luxury perfume can be worth a pretty penny on Ebay, even if the bottle is nearly used up.

Note that fragrances from high-end names are not the only ones to look for. Bath & Body Works and Victoria's Secret scents do well on Ebay, especially because they retire lines frequently, making discontinued items even more sought after. And because those two retailers sell different lines of products in different countries, people outside of America are looking to get their hands-on scents only sold here. Again, be sure to open your sales up internationally through Ebay's Global Shipping program for easy shipping to overseas customers.

When selling perfume on Ebay, be aware that it has to ship via ground, not Priority (i.e., by truck or boat, not airplane). This is due to the alcohol content, which can be flammable at high altitudes. Be sure to only list perfumes Parcel Post, not Priority or First Class. Most perfumes are under 16 ounces, but they still can NOT ship First Class mail, only Parcel. Because we ship many items via Parcel Post, we keep a wide variety of different sized cardboard boxes on hand, including small boxes for perfumes.

One of my favorite finds ever was a small set of three perfumes that I bought for 50-cents; I sold each individually and profited nearly $60! Be sure to disclose the bottle size of perfumes in your listings, along with pictures of the bottle and cap. Also, be honest about how much liquid is still in the bottle. Half-empty bottles do sell, so tell customers up front what they are buying. Also, be clear about the bottle size. Sometimes tiny bottles appear to be full size in photos, so you want to make sure buyers know the actual size.

Wrap perfume bottles well for shipment. We wrap them in bubble wrap, and we tape the bubble wrap to ensure the cap does not come off. We then put the bubble-wrapped bottle into a plastic bag and surround it with lots of packing paper in the box to prevent the bottle from breaking during transit.

#66 PET COSTUMES

C hildren's Halloween costumes sell well on Ebay, but pet costumes sell REALLY well! This is one item I will buy new to resell as they can go as low as 90% off after Halloween at the big box retailers. I have been able to get the full retail price for them on Ebay, and they sell all year long as people are always looking to dress their dogs and cats up for some occasion. Doggie wedding dresses are especially popular!

I have dogs myself, so I know the mess they can make, especially if they shed. That is why I am very careful about picking up used pet costumes to resell. If I do get them, they have to be in excellent condition, and I always wash them to make sure there is no hair on them.

As I mentioned, it can be worth browsing the clearance section at the big box stores and pet stores for costumes on clearance. Be careful about paying too much, though, as you want to maximize your profits. As I said, I only buy pet costumes to resell if they are 90% off. If I can find a $10 outfit on clearance for $1, I will likely pick it up. And I will get as many as I can so that I can create one listing with multiple outfits available in each size.

When listing dog costumes, it is very important to note the size accurately as some brands only design for small breeds yet have sizes ranging from extra small to extra-large. My dogs are pugs, which is a small toy breed. However, in many pet costume sizes, they wear larges as the clothes run really small.

The sizing is another reason why I like to stick to only carrying new pet costumes, as the package information clearly states the measurements.

Pet costumes that are new in the package are fast and easy to list as you only need a photo of the back and the front, and you can copy all of the information from the package right into your listing. Because these costumes are lightweight and usually weigh under 16 ounces, you can often ship them in poly mailers or bubble envelopes at the First-Class rate.

#67 POSTCARDS

In addition to collecting John Deere toys and matchbooks, for years, my dad also collected postcards. As I had done with his matchbooks, when he was done with collecting postcards, I sold them on Ebay for a nice amount. Since he had gotten most of them for free during vacations, most of the money he made was pure profit.

Like matchbooks, postcards are another item people tend to markup rather high at garage and estate sales. They themselves likely have been collecting them and paying for them individually, so they are looking to make their money back. And while there are postcards that sell for a high amount on their own, I only buy them to resell on Ebay if there are a large number bundled together for a super low price.

Because there are cards that sell well on their own, many sellers on Ebay do piece them out and sell them one by one. These sellers usually only deal in postcards; however; so not only are they extremely knowledgeable on what cards are worth, but they also do not mind having mostly $1 to $3 sales.

I prefer to lot postcards together and sell them in big bundles. Not only can I charge more for dozens of postcards in one lot, but it makes listing and shipping them much easier. Usually, I just spread the postcards out on a table and take one picture of them, letting the buyer have the fun of getting their package and sorting through all of the cards, looking for potential treasures.

However, you can also sort postcards out by theme or location and sell them that way.

Postcards are a lightweight item that can ship via First Class mail in a bubble mailer as long as the weight does not exceed 16 ounces. If you have a pile of cards that weighs over a pound, you can ship them in a Priority Mail Flat Rate Bubble Mailer. I like to put postcards in a plastic zipper bag, seal the bag, and then slide the bag into the mailing envelope. This ensures the cards stay together and do not fall out everywhere when the buyer opens the envelope.

#68 PLUS SIZE CLOTHING

If there is one general rule of thumb for reselling clothing, it is the bigger, the better! Larger sizes sell out first in the stores, making them highly desirable on Ebay. When it comes to plus size clothing for men and women, the brand is not as important as people who wear 3X or larger have fewer brands to choose from in the first place.

Thankfully, my Goodwill hangs clothing on the racks according to size, making it easy to find the larger sizes. When I go into Goodwill, my first stop is always the big and tall men's section. I look for anything sized extra-large or bigger. And while size trumps brand when it comes to larger sizes, the condition is still important. So be sure to check for stains and rips just as you would on any clothing you are buying to resell on Ebay.

Note that larger sizes and the term "plus-size" are not always the same. Most clothing brands sell sizes extra small to 2XL and market them as "regular size." However, some brands then produce "plus-size," which is actually different. For instance, Old Navy has size 2XL jackets in the "regular size,"; but then they also have 2XL jackets in their "plus-size" range. I always do a Google search on a brand before I list it on Ebay, so I am sure exactly what the sizing means.

We wash and iron most clothes before listing them on Ebay. This ensures the clothing is free of that "thrift store" smell or from the odors of the previous owner. We also iron down collars and cuffs that are not hanging flat, and we often have to iron men's shirts. I take photos of the front of the piece of clothing and the back, plus an up-close shot of the collar and tag area. If there are any special details on the garment (buttons, pockets, hood, belt, etc.), I take pictures of those, too.

When listing clothing on Ebay, it is important to take correct measurements. I provide three measurements in all shirt listings, taken by laying the garment flat out on a table: pit to pit (tape measure drawn from under one armpit to the other), sleeve (tape measure drawn from the shoulder seam to the cuff; or from the collar to the cuff if there is no seam, with that difference noted in the listing), and body length (tape measure drawn from the collar to the hem). For pants, I measure the waist and the inseam.

The best part of selling clothing is how easy it is to ship. Since plus size clothing has more fabric, it is often heavier than 16 ounces, meaning it needs to go either Parcel Select or Priority Mail. I have poly bags and bubble mailers on hand just for clothing. The Post Office has Flat Rate Priority Mail bubble mailers that are perfect for shipping out clothes. To help clothes slide easily into the bubble mailers, we roll them up and put them into poly bags first, and we then put the polybag into the bubble envelope.

#69 PUFFER JACKETS & VESTS

G oing through the coat rack at the thrift store can be overwhelming, but two items to quickly scan for are puffer jackets and vests. Characterized by puffed quilted material, these pieces of outerwear sell very well on Ebay, even from such brands as Old Navy. A Gap puffer vest in a larger size is almost always an easy $30 on Ebay.

My Goodwill not only hangs puffer jackets and vests in the coat section but also in the women's blazer section and sometimes even on a small little rack with other vests. Fortunately, puffer vests are easy to spot, even from a distance.

As with all clothing, larger sizes tend to sell faster; but with puffer vests, I have had good luck selling even the small adult sizes as well as children's sizes. While I do not pick up brands that are sold at Walmart or Target, I do pick up inexpensive mall brands of puffer vests such as those from Old Navy and Christopher & Banks.

Note the materials printed on the label of the garment and include them in your Ebay listing. Often puffer jackets have a nylon shell and a polyester lining, but some are down-filled. I have had a puffer vest with a nylon shell, a down fill, and a fleece collar. Buyers will want to know the exact materials, as well as all features such as any pockets or a hood.

For puffer vests, I take a picture of the front and back, along with an up-close picture of the collar and tag area. I then take a picture of the piece opened up to show the lining. Be sure to note if the jacket has a zipper, snaps, or a combination of both. It is not uncommon for the higher end brands to have a snap panel over a zipper.

When listing clothing on Ebay, it's important to take correct measurements. I provide three measurements for puffer jackets and vest, taken by laying the garment flat out on a table: pit to pit (tape measure drawn from under one armpit to the other), sleeve (tape measure drawn from the shoulder seam to the cuff; or from the collar to the cuff if there is no seam), and body length (tape measure drawn from the collar to the hem).

Puffer vests can be shipped in a polybag or bubble mailer, although we avoid rolling them up and stuffing them in a Flat Rate Bubble envelope as that just looks bag to the customer. Lightweight puffer vests can ship via First Class if the package weighs under 16 ounces. If they are over 16 ounces, we ship them in a polybag via Priority as the shipping discount I get on Ebay usually comes out costing less than Parcel Select. You can get a free roll of Priority Mail stickers from the Post Office to put on plain bags or boxes that you are using to ship Priority packages.

#70 PUFF THE MAGIC DRAGON

While many people associate "Puff, The Magic Dragon" with the cartoon films released in the late 1970s, Puff actually originated as a 1963 song from the group Peter, Paul, and Mary. The lyrics for the song were based on a 1959 poem by Leonard Lipton, who was inspired by the Ogden Nash poem "Custard the Dragon."

While many have speculated that the poem and song contain drug references, the artists have always maintained it is simply a tale of children outgrowing their imaginations and their loss of innocence. As the boy in the song grows up, he loses his belief in Puff; and Puff is left alone.

When it comes to selling "Puff, the Magic Dragon" items on Ebay, note that it is the cartoon items you will want to be on the lookout for. I once picked up a small vintage Puff the Magic Dragon stuffed toy at an estate sale for 50-cents. It sold quickly on Ebay for $24.99, and the buyer paid for the shipping. Puff the Magic Dragon merchandise is pretty scarce, so if you find it cheap and in good condition, snatch it up.

#71 PYREX DISHES

Vintage Pyrex mixing bowls are extremely collectible but also very hard to find in good condition. I see a lot of Pyrex at estate sales, but it is usually priced high and gets snatched up fast. The ones that are leftover often have too much wear to resell on Ebay.

Pink is the most popular Pyrex color and the hardest to find. There are also very rare prints that can command thousands of dollars on Ebay. It is worth your time to study the completed Pyrex listings on Ebay to educate yourself on the desired patterns and their price points.

There are lots of various Pyrex pieces besides mixing bowls, including mugs, which I frequently find at estate sales. The mugs do sell but not for much. They also sell better in lots, but then you have the challenge of shipping a large box of ceramics. I generally avoid the mugs and just keep an eye out for the bowls, specifically, the nesting bowls, which are various sizes of bowls meant to stack together. Certain casserole dishes complete with their glass lids can also bring in a pretty penny on Ebay.

Be sure the Pyrex pieces you pick up are in good condition and that the color has not faded. I have made the mistake of selling a piece where the print was very worn, and the buyer immediately demanded a refund.

Because of their heavyweight, I list Pyrex using calculated shipping with the buyer paying the postage cost. Trying to build "free" shipping into the price of Pyrex inflates the sale price to a ridiculous level. Be sure to take care when packaging Pyrex for shipping by using a lot of bubble wrap and plenty of packing paper or peanuts. These pieces are extremely fragile, so we tend to go overboard with packing materials just to be on the safe side.

#72 RALPH LAUREN CLOTHING

I f there is one brand of men's clothing that I always look for at thrift stores, it is Ralph Lauren as it is a consistent seller on Ebay. I always make sure to look in the women's section for plus size Lauren by Ralph Lauren shirts and jackets, too. Ralph Lauren also produces children's clothing, which is wildly expensive new, even at their outlet stores; therefore, finding it secondhand is always a great score.

There are several styles produced under the Ralph Lauren name, with Polo by Ralph Lauren being the most desirable in terms of selling it on Ebay. I can often pick up simple solid color polo shirts under the Polo by Ralph Lauren name for as little as $1 at a Goodwill sale, and they easily sell for $15.99 with free shipping on Ebay. More colorful designs and higher quality shirts and sweaters sell for much more.

Finding vintage Ralph Lauren POLO rugby shirts is also very exciting as these pieces bring the most money. Ralph Lauren has been making the Olympic outfits for U.S. athletes for several years now, and those pieces can bring in over $1000 on Ebay.

Note that Ralph Lauren used to produce a Chaps by Ralph Lauren line. These pieces generally do not sell well on Ebay as eventually, Lauren sold the brand, and it is now sold at Kohls. Also, there is a brand of clothing called U.S. Polo Association that often gets mistaken for Polo by Ralph Lauren; however, it is not Ralph Lauren and does not sell well on Ebay. Make sure "Ralph Lauren" is actually on the tag of any piece you are considering buying for Ebay.

In addition to shirts, also look for hats, tee shirts, purses, and tote bags bearing the Ralph Lauren pony logo. Ralph Lauren also makes men's pants and shorts; shoes, sweaters, coats, and jackets for both men and women; skirts and dresses for women; and clothing, shoes, and accessories for babies and children.

As with all clothing, be sure to check for stains and rips. Damaged Ralph Lauren clothing is not desirable, so only pick up pieces in good, clean condition. We wash and iron most clothes before listing them on Ebay; while an entire shirt may not need ironing, often the collars and cuffs of shirts do so that they will lay flat for photos. I take pictures of the front of the piece of clothing and the back, plus an up-close shot of the collar and tag area. If there are any special details on the garment (buttons, pockets, zippers, belt, hood), I take pictures of those, too.

As I have already mentioned several times, when listing clothing on Ebay, it is important to take correct measurements. I provide three measurements in all shirt and jacket listings, taken by laying the garment flat out on a table: pit to pit (tape measure drawn from under one armpit to the other), sleeve (tape measure drawn from the shoulder seam to the cuff; or from the collar to the cuff if there is no seam), and body length (tape measure drawn from the collar to the hem). For pants, I take the waist measurements as well as the inseam.

We ship Ralph Lauren clothing that weighs under 16 ounces via First Class in poly envelopes. For heavier pieces, we roll them up, wrap them in packing paper or a plain polybag, and put them into a Priority Mail Flat Rate Bubble Mailer.

#73 ROYAL FAMILY SOUVENIRS

E ngland produces all kinds of memorabilia for Royal weddings and the Royal families, although it is hard to find in the States. From Princess Di and Charles to Will and Kate, these are nice items to pick up to resell on Ebay if you find them while out picking.

I usually find Royals souvenirs at estate sales. When Princess Diane married Prince Charles, there was a lot of promotional merchandise available to order via television and magazine ads, which many people in the States purchased. I also find items that people have picked up on European vacations and cruises.

Royal merchandise may not bring a lot of money – I've gotten $10 for a Diane and Charles mug as well as $10 for a mug featuring Fergie and Andrew – but they are usually cheap to pick up at sales, and they are a fun item to have in your merchandise mix. Note that I only pick up Royals items that were produced in England; pieces marked "Made in China" are not authorized by the Royal family and are not going to sell well on Ebay.

Princess Diana remains the most popular Royal, with dolls bearing her likeness selling very well on Ebay. There is also a Princess Diana purple Beanie Baby that can go for big bucks depending on the issue, country of manufacture, and the filling. Overall, Beanie Babies do NOT sell on Ebay (or anywhere else, for that matter, as the once-hot tread was mass-produced and quickly died out). However, it is worth your time to study the completed Ebay listings for Princess Diana Beanie Babies (as well as all Beanie Babies) to educate yourself on which ones to look for.

#74 SCRABBLE TILES

When I spot a pile of board games at Goodwill or an estate sale, I always do a quick scan to see if there are any Scrabble sets. Crafters, especially scrapbookers and jewelry makers, love to use the Scrabble tiles in their projects.

The going rate on Ebay for a set of Scrabble tiles is around $10 for 100 tiles. Instead of selling these in lots of 100, however, I like to save up as many as I can to sell in one large lot. The maroon color tiles bring in a bit more than the standard beige ones, but the price of both has dropped in recent years. Still, if you can pick up Scrabble games cheap, the tiles make for a nice little sale on Ebay.

In addition to the tiles, the Scrabble tile trays and boards also sell. Crafters use the trays in various projects, and some people craft books out of the boards. Also, organizers of Scrabble tournaments are always looking for extra trays and boards; so, there is a market out there for these pieces. As with the tiles, I save up the trays and boards until I have a good size lot of them.

To list Scrabble tiles, I usually just take one photo of the entire pile. I also put the exact number of titles in the listing (unless they are still new and sealed in their original bag, you will want to count them twice to ensure accuracy).

Since $10 is a going rate per 100 tiles, I list these using calculated shipping with the customer paying the shipping cost. You can fit several bags of tiles into a Priority Mail Flat Rate Bubble Mailer and ship them anywhere in the United States for less than $8.

#75 SCRAP FLATWARE

Earlier I talked about silverware sets being strong sellers on Ebay, but do not overlook those random pieces of flatware that you find in the bins at thrift stores or in bags at estate sales. I frequently find little plastic bags of miscellaneous flatware at estate sales for as little as 25-cents, and I always snatch them up.

I look for spoons and forks with decorative handles as jewelry makers bend these to make rings and bracelets. I keep a Priority Mail Flat Rate box in my office and toss in random flatware as I find it. Once the box is full, I sell it for $99.99 on Ebay with free shipping.

Be sure to check for sterling silver marks on the pieces first, as real silver is very valuable on its own. I have only found silver plate and stainless thus far in my picking journey, but one never knows when they might get lucky! This is another reason why people like to buy random scrap flatware: they are hoping to find sterling.

When we sell sets of flatware, we like to polish them up nicely in order to maximize the asking price. And while we do not take as much time with scrap flatware, we do wash them and polish extremely tarnished pieces.

To list these scrap flatware lots, I like to spread the pieces out on a table and take one photo of the entire lot together. This way, the customer has a general idea of what they are buying, but they will not know each piece exactly until they get their package.

To ship, we put the flatware into a plastic bag and then use packing paper to secure the bag inside of the box. The Medium Flat Rate Priority Mail box currently ships for under $14, so even after the price I spent to buy the flatware and then paying for shipping, I am still left with a nice profit that I did not have to work too hard for.

#76 SECONDARY DISNEY CHARACTERS

E veryone knows the Walt Disney characters Mickey Mouse and Minnie Mouse, and you can find merchandise with their likenesses on it everywhere. But it is the secondary Disney character products featuring Donald Duck, Pluto, Goofy, and supporting characters from Disney movies that are harder to find and therefore more valuable for resale on Ebay.

Years ago, I bought up a bunch of Cheshire Cat plush toys from "Alice In Wonderland" at a Disney Outlet Store. They were on clearance, so I only paid a couple of bucks each, and I was able to resell them quickly on Ebay for $15 apiece with the buyers all paying shipping. Also, I once found a box of Disney antenna toppers at a garage sale for 25-cents each. I bought the whole box, and some of the lesser-known characters ended up selling for over $20 on Ebay. I have also picked up Disney Hallmark ornaments featuring Jiminy Cricket that sold for over their original asking price.

Disney has licenses on a wide variety of products, including clothing, coffee mugs, bedding, collectibles, and toys. Ebay has an entire "Disneyana" sub-category under the "Collectible" category as the number of Disney products available is so large that they command an entire section of the site. And while Mickey and Minnie mouse items will still sell on Ebay, you will almost always make more on the secondary characters (unless you have a rare vintage piece).

Even Disney movies that do not end up being big box office hits still have a character or two in them that collectors fall in love with. Older movies especially do not have much merchandise available to purchase new (think "Dumbo" and "Bambi"). If you find an item with a "Disney" mark on it and a character you do not recognize, chances are it is a rarer product that might bring in the big bucks on Ebay!

#77 PRIVATE COLLEGE MERCHANDISE

E very state has an array of small, private colleges. If you look around at your local thrift stores and garage sales, you will likely spot coffee mugs and clothing items from these schools. And I have found these items sell very well on Ebay, even better than items from the larger state universities.

Not only do these small, private institutions produce less merchandise than the big colleges, but their graduates also tend to be more spread out throughout the country. While a local state college may get the majority of students from the nearby surrounding area, private schools attract kids from across the country; many of whom do not stay in the state after graduation. It is these graduates, who now live across the country, who love to buy up memorabilia from their collegiate days.

A simple coffee mug from a private college is usually an easy $10 sale on Ebay (I often pick these up at estate sales for only a quarter), while nice coats and jackets embroidered with the school logo start at $25 and go up depending on condition and size. In addition to clothes and mugs, be on the lookout for ceramic steins with college logos.

Memorabilia is not just limited to mugs and clothes, though. I often find awards, trophies, yearbooks, pins, patches, and pens from small schools at estate sales, as the homeowners or their children had attended private colleges both in Iowa and around the country. These items are almost always leftover on the last day of sales, meaning I can snag them for at least 50% off (or practically nothing if the estate sale company is running a fill-a-bag sale).

As with anything you buy to resell on Ebay, make sure items are in good condition before buying them to resell. Look for chips, cracks, and spoon marks on ceramics, and check for stains and tears on clothing. Take plenty of photos and describe items accurately to get the highest selling price and to ensure a happy customer.

You have two category choices when listing college souvenirs on Ebay: The NCAA subcategory under the "Sports Mem, Card & Fan Shop" category; OR under the "Colleges & Universities" subcategory under the "Collectibles – Historical Memorabilia – Teaching & Education" category. If the product is not related to a sporting team, I will list it under "Colleges & Universities." The exception to this is for items from schools with a large athletic following or with teams currently doing extremely well on the national level (i.e., they are headed to a big bowl football game or are in the basketball playoffs).

#78 SLIDE RULERS

Drafting supplies such as slide rulers bring a lot of money on Ebay, especially if they come with their original cases and instructions. While most of these items tend to sell best in lots, even a slide ruler on its own can fetch around $10 online. I like to save slide rulers up until I have several to sell together in order to get the most amount of money.

Note that slide rulers are not a very common thing to find at sales and thrift stores; I usually spot them every now and then at an estate sale. The good thing is that usually, where there is one slide ruler, there are others as the person selling them had several. Most people do not know the value of these on Ebay, so you can usually get them pretty cheap. Putting two or more rulers together in one lot will sell much better and much faster than a single ruler. And rulers that come with their original paperwork and cases sell for a lot more than a single ruler on its own.

I once was at the estate sale of a former auctioneer who had a basement full of treasures, including old drafting supplies. I bought two vintage slide rulers, both with their original cases and instructions, for $4. They told together on Ebay for $50 with the buyer paying shipping.

Be careful when shipping these rulers as you do not want them to break during transit. While it is tempting to put a ruler in a bubble mailer, it is much safer to ship them in a small box to avoid them being snapped in half. If you do ship them in an envelope, make sure to use plenty of bubble wrap so that the package cannot be bent.

#79 SONY WALKMANS

Portable radios with cassette or CD players from the '80s and '90s are hot sellers today on Ebay as not everyone has made the leap to MP3 players. Sony is an especially hot seller online; so, if you spot a Sony Walkman for a good price, snatch it up.

I always make sure any electronics, including Walkman's, are in good, working condition. We keep a supply of different batteries on hand for testing products, and you will also want to have a cassette on hand to test Walkman's to ensure the music comes through. If you find Sony Walkman's that are not in working condition, you can still sell them for parts.

Be sure to check the battery compartments of any Walkman's you are considering buying (as well as all electronic items) to ensure they do not have damage from battery erosion. I like to include a photo of the battery compartment so that customers know the condition. While I do test units with batteries, I do not include batteries with the order as they are expensive and add extra weight. I add a simple "Tested with fresh batteries, but batteries are not included" statement in the listing.

Note that these Walkman's may or may not come with their original headphones, but the headphones are not nearly as important as the unit itself; it is perfectly fine to buy and resell Walkman's without headphones. In fact, because many people now use earbuds or special headphones, the original headphones likely will not even be used. However, you will want to make sure you do have headphones on hand to test any Walkman before you list it on Ebay.

Wrapped up well in bubble wrap, you can ship a Sony Walkman in a Priority Mail Flat Rate Bubble Mailer. However, if the original headphones are included, I would advise shipping these in a box as the headphones could snap during transit. Most of these Walkman's and their headphones fit comfortably into the 7x7x6 Priority Mail box. These usually weigh over a pound what boxed for shipment, so these are items that I usually list using calculated shipping so that the buyer pays the postage cost.

#80 STARBUCKS COFFEE MUGS

I love picking up coffee mugs to resell on Ebay. They are one of the few items that you can find for as little as 10-cents and flip for $10. However, just because SOME coffee mugs sell on Ebay does not mean they all do. In fact, MOST coffee mugs you see at garage sales and thrift stores will not sell online.

This is a common mistake I see many new Ebay sellers make. They hear about a category of items that sell and buy up every item they see that fits into that category. However, it is not about the category as a whole, but the individual brands and styles. MOST things you find secondhand do NOT sell on Ebay. Being a successful Ebay seller is all about learning to find the hidden gems in the vast piles of junk.

As for coffee mugs, there is one BRAND that is always a good pick up to sell on Ebay; and that is Starbucks. Starbucks has issued and continues to release a wide variety of ceramic coffee mugs for holidays, events, and their various store locations.

In terms of picking up Starbucks mugs to sell on Ebay, the older the style, the better. And mugs from specific states or cities are particularly desirable as you can usually only buy them at stores in those areas. However, even a basic ceramic white cup with the green Starbucks logo on it is an easy $10 on Ebay.

As with all mugs, I make sure they are in great condition with no chips, cracks, spoon marks, or scratching of the logo. Starbucks mugs are clearly marked as such on the bottom. And while I normally shy away from products stamped as "Made in China," in the case of Starbucks mugs, the country of manufacture is not important.

To list Starbucks mugs on Ebay, I take photos of all four sides of the mug as well as the bottom and a shot looking down into the mug. If the name of the design is not clear, I simply do a search on Ebay for a similar style to find the name. In the listing, I include the measurements for the height of the mug as well as for the mouth (the opening at the top where you drink out of).

We almost always ship coffee mugs in the 7x7x6 Priority Mail boxes. Since I pay and print for my labels online, Priority usually cost less than Parcel as the Post Office offers an online shipping discount. Plus, I can then use a free Priority Mail box from the Post Office. My dad, who handles the shipping, wraps mugs in several layers of bubble wrap and then fashions a cardboard sleeve around it before surrounding it with packing paper in the box. Yes, this is a lot of packing material for a small item; be we have never had a mug break during shipment using this method.

#81 STARTER BRAND SPORTS JACKETS

S tarter is a pricey brand of coats, jackets, and athletic wear, and while there are a lot of basic Starter clothing pieces at the thrift stores, the best ones to sell on Ebay are the parka coats from various sports teams. Whether it is from the NFL, NBA, NHL, or NCAA, if I can find a big winter parker from Starter for $5 or less, I pick it up as it will sell for $40 or more on Ebay.

I often find coats with missing hoods, however, which I am careful to disclose in the listing. A missing hood will affect the price, so unless it is a super-hot team, I usually do not pick up coats with missing hoods.

These coats are expensive new, so often they end up at the thrift stores because they have damage. It is important to inspect these garments closely for stains and rips. I recently picked up a Chicago Bulls Starter jacket for $2 that looked to be in excellent condition. However, when I got it home, I found a giant hole under the arm.

I list team apparel in the "Fan Apparel & Souvenirs" Ebay subcategory, which is under the "Sports Mem, Cards & Fan Shop" main category. From there, you can narrow down the category further for NCAA, NFL, NBA, and so on. You can then choose the team from the item's specifics list located within the listing.

I measure coats the same way I measure shirts, taken by laying the garment flat out on a table: pit to pit (tape measure is drawn from under one armpit to the other), sleeve (tape measure drawn from the shoulder seam to the cuff; or from the collar to the cuff if there is no seam), and body length (tape measure drawn from the collar to the hem). I also make sure to point out pockets, whether the coat zips or snaps, and the material. I take a photo of the front, a photo of the back, an up-close photo of the collar/tag area, and a few more photos of other details, such as the embroidered logos.

Because these parkas are big and bulky, we ship them in large poly envelopes. While these bags are very sturdy and not prone to tearing, we do wrap the coats up in some packing paper to give them added protection during transit. These coats can weigh quite a bit, so we check both the Parcel Select price and the Priority Mail price to see which is less. As always, if Priority only costs a bit more, I upgrade the order to the faster shipping time.

#82 TERVIS
TUMBLERS

Y ou have likely seen Tervis Tumblers at gift shops; they are clear plastic thermal glasses with embroidered patches inside of them. Tervis Tumblers are rather pricey ($15 for a plastic cup), but they are also very collectible, which makes them a great item to pick up secondhand to resell on Ebay. In fact, Tervis Tumblers have been around a long time, and the vintage ones are very sought after.

I found out personally how hot a commodity vintage Tervis Tumblers were when I picked up three small glasses at an estate sale. They each had a simple holly berry Christmas design to them; they had definitely been used and even had some cracks. However, since I arrived during the $5 fill-a-bag event towards the end of the sale, I just threw them in my bag. I listed these used, beat up cups at auction; and they went for $14. That same year, I found three more vintage Tervis cups with a glitter confetti design; I paid 25-cents each. Little did I know that these are the most sought-after cups by collectors. I sold all three glasses for a total of $40!

Note that there are lots of knock-off Tervis Tumblers out there, so be sure to check the bottoms of the glasses before you buy them to resell on Ebay. All Tervis products are marked as such on the bottom. Take several photos for your listing, and do not overstate the condition. Collectors will buy glasses that have scuffs and cracks, but if you list a glass in like-new condition and it is not, your buyer will likely open up a case against you. Collectors are notoriously hard to please, so to be safe, I always understate the condition of the products I sell on Ebay.

While plastic glasses likely are not going to break during shipment, it is still important to wrap Tervis Tumblers in bubble wrap and to use plenty of packing material to protect them during transit. The tall glasses fit nicely inside of the Priority Mail Shoe Box, while the shorter tumblers go into the 7x7x6 size box. If I am selling several cups, I usually end up using the large 12x12x8 Priority box.

#83 THERMOS STANLEY CONTAINERS FROM ALLADIN

T hermos branded thermal hot/cold containers are an item you can usually find for less than $1 at garage sales. You can sell them individually, or you can lot them together. I find selling them in lots to be much easier as well as more cost-effective for shipping. Since one of these can weigh up to 3 pounds on its own when packaged, the shipping can sometimes be more than the selling price of the actual thermos.

I make sure to only buy thermos products that are marked as Aladdin Thermos Stanley as these are the authentic brand that collectors are after. I also only buy ones that are in very good condition with no cracks, dents, or rust. And I only buy pieces that are complete with their caps, both the twist-on cap and the drinking cup. Condition is very important when it comes to selling Thermos on Ebay; so, pass up any you see that are not in excellent shape.

I love finding the vintage Thermos sets in picnic cases, which come in a bag and have several cups and containers. Sets in leather bags can fetch upwards of $100 on Ebay. Harder to find are the vintage children's metal lunchboxes with a thermos container that Aladdin produced featuring cartoons and television shows. It is no secret that these lunchboxes are highly collectible and command a high price on Ebay, but if you see a Thermos without the matching lunchbox, still pick it up. Many thermoses and lunchboxes became separated, meaning collectors are looking to find the missing thermos to their lunchbox.

Probably the most famous Thermos pattern is the red plaid design. One of these in excellent condition can bring $25 on its own on Ebay. While red is the most common color, some of these were produced in blue and also in beige.

When listing Thermos products, it is important to put all the information found on the bottom of the thermos into the listing as collectors can be very fussy about the size of these. There are several pieces to these thermoses, and each part will be listed on the bottom of the thermos. Don't worry if you cannot understand exactly what the numbers mean; just copy them as-is into your listing. Make sure to take photos of the outside as well as the bottom plus an inside shot looking down into the thermos.

Thermoses fit perfectly into the USPS Priority Mail Shoe Box. Because these are often over 2 pounds, I list these using calculated shipping so that the buyer pays the cost to have it delivered to their zip code. Because these pieces are prone to cracking, be sure to wrap them in bubble wrap and to use packing paper to protect them during transit.

#84 THOMAS
THE TRAIN

Thomas the Train is a hot toy, and one that is also crazy expensive! When my great-nephew was really into Thomas & Friends, I had a hard time finding an affordable gift from the line to give him. That is why anything Thomas is a hot seller on Ebay.

It is not only the Thomas branded toy trains that sell on Ebay, but also the track pieces and accessories. Not to mention all of the bedding, lamps, accessories, clothing, and books that are also on the market. Thomas items are plentiful at garage sales as children outgrow them.

Note that there are both metal Thomas trains and wooden ones. Both sell well, but the wood pieces sell extremely well. Many sets are now made of plastic, which has only driven up demand for the wood ones. Regardless of the material, the more Thomas items you have to sell, the better. Parents who turn to Ebay for Thomas products are looking for big lots of trains and track pieces to buy. So, if you are only finding single Thomas trains when you are out picking, consider saving them up until you have a nice lot to list. Of course, be sure to do a completed listing search of any Thomas items you find, as there are some that are extremely valuable on their own.

I love to list lots of similar items on Ebay as it is so much easier than listing things one by one. For a large lot of Thomas train pieces, lay them all out and get a shot of the entire lot. Then just zoom in to take pictures of several groupings to give buyers an up-close look at everything included. You usually do not have to be as meticulous in listing lots as you would be listing individual pieces; just list the number of train cars and the number of pieces of track. The buyer will then have to sort everything out.

Because of the weight of the train cars and track pieces, you will want to make sure to list these using calculated shipping, with the buyer paying the postage cost to their zip code. Make sure you have a box on hand to ship all of the pieces; you will likely end up sending these via Parcel Post due to the weight, so you will need a plain cardboard box for shipping. Putting the track pieces in a plastic bag and then using packing paper to wrap each train car will ensure the entire lot arrives safely to the buyer.

#85 TOMMY BAHAMA CLOTHING

With so many clothing brands being produced today, it can be overwhelming to figure out which ones sell well on Ebay. And even though a certain style of a brand may sell, it does not mean every piece from that designer will. However, one brand that is a sure thing to resell on Ebay is Tommy Bahama!

Tommy Bahama is a high-end brand of resort and golf wear. While they do produce women's clothing, I mostly come across men's tops at the thrift stores. The two main pieces of Tommy Bahama men's clothing I find are short sleeve button front Hawaiian shirts and golf sweater vests. I have sold their golf sweater vests for $19.99 each, a great profit margin considering I only paid $2 for them at a garage sale. And I have sold the Hawaiian shirts for as much as $40, again only paying a dollar or two for them.

While larger size clothing usually does best on Ebay, I have sold all sizes of Tommy Bahama, from small to extra-large. Before buying Tommy Bahama clothes to resell, be sure to look them over for stains or rips; and check the buttons to make sure they are all intact. Also, make sure the size tag has not been cut out.

I've mentioned before that we wash all clothing before listing it on Ebay, and for Tommy Bahama button-front shirts, we may end up needing to iron them (although these are not prone to wrinkles, so sometimes we only need to iron the collar down). I take three photos of shirts: front, back, and an up-close shot of the collar/tag area.

I provide three measurements in all shirt listings, taken by laying the garment flat out on a table: pit to pit (tape measure drawn from under one armpit to the other), sleeve (tape measure drawn from the shoulder seam to the cuff; or from the collar to the cuff if there is no seam), and body length (tape measure drawn from the collar to the hem). Note that for short sleeve shirts, I skip the sleeve measurement and only provide the pit-to-pit and length numbers.

Most Tommy Bahama Hawaiian shirts are light enough to ship via First Class Mail in poly envelopes. For heavier sweaters, we roll them up, wrap them in packing paper or a plain polybag, and then slide them into a Priority Mail Flat Rate Bubble Mailer.

#86 TRAVEL
TIN PLATES

T ravel souvenir items can be hit or miss to resell on Ebay. After all, most people want to pick up their own vacation memorabilia, not buy someone else's. However, there are some travel items that DO sell, including vintage round tin plates representing the various United States of America.

These black metal plates are approximately 11-inches in diameter and feature colorful illustrations of a state's main cities and attractions, such as the state of Florida with Disney World, Sea World, and the Space Center featured prominently. Do a "Sold" completed listing search for "Tin Souvenir Travel Plate" on Ebay to see what these tins look like (you will also see what types of other travel plates to keep an eye out for).

I can usually pick these plates up for as little as a quarter at estate sales and sell them for $9.99. Not a big sale, I know, but it is these small sales that really make up the bread and butter of an Ebay business. While these plates will sell on their own, they sell even better in lots as collectors are usually trying to get all of the States. So, you may want to save these up until you have four or five to put together in one listing.

Finding these tin plates in good condition is a challenge as many are dented and rusty. However, they do not have to be in mint condition to sell, as some scratches on the back are common due to the material. However, I pass up any with major condition issues as they are not going to sell with excessive dents, rust, and scratches.

I list these plates in the "Souvenirs & Travel Memorabilia" subcategory under the "Collectibles" category. I take two photos: one of the front-side of the plate and one of the back-side.

These are lightweight plates but resist the urge to put them in an envelope to ship. Because these plates are susceptible to dents, you will want to package them in a box for safe shipment. These usually fit in a rectangular Priority Mail box, often weighing less than a pound ship. Or if you have a plain cardboard box, they may weigh under 16 ounces when packaged, meaning you can ship them via First Class Mail.

While you do not have to go overboard with packing material, you will still want to use a bit of packing paper to protect the plate during transit. And good packaging practices are always rewarded when it comes to customers, leaving you positive feedback.

#87 TUBE RADIOS

Vintage tube radios (also called vacuum tube radios) are characterized as devices that control the electric current through a vacuum in a sealed container. Tube radios from the '50s and '60s can usually be picked up for cheap and are quick sellers on Ebay, depending on the condition, shape, and color. The mid-century modern styles with their clean lines are particularly hot sellers on Ebay.

While these radios sell best in working condition, you can still sell broken ones "as is" for parts. While larger, antique models can sell for hundreds of dollars, you will likely be picking up tabletop units that sell in the $25 to $50 range. Good brands to look for are Zenith, RCA, and General Electric. This is another Ebay category that is worth your time to study, so you will have a good idea of what to look for. Simply do a "Sold" completed listing search for "vintage tube radios" to analyze the results.

Some of these radios have Bakelite shells; so, if you pick up a unit that is plastic on the outside, be sure to test it for Bakelite as these are highly desirable. Simply dip a cotton swab into a bit of Simi chrome polish (which is a non-abrasive cream that we keep on hand to clean metal) and run on the material you are testing. Simi chrome polish is pink, but it will turn yellow if the piece is Bakelite. A tube or jar of Simi chrome polish is just another product to keep in your Ebay tool kit; you can find it with the cleaning products at most big box stores.

The only downside to shipping tube radios is that they tend to be heavy and bulky, which can make the postage a bit expensive. While the shipping on these radios can run a bit high, my buyers have always gladly paid the shipping cost to get the radio they wanted. This is the type of item I list using calculated shipping, so the buyer pays the shipping cost to their location. These radios often fit in the large 12x12x8 Priority Mail boxes, although we also have plain cardboard boxes on hand to ship via Parcel Post if that service is less. We use plenty of bubble wrap and packing paper to protect them during transit.

Prices vary widely in this category, with some models fetching thousands of dollars, although the ones I have found have sold anywhere from $20-60. Considering that they can be found at most estate sales and thrift stores for as little as $1, tube radios are a great item to add to your list of items to look for when out picking!

#88 TV SHOW COFFEE MUGS

For people who visit New York or L.A., a trip to see a television show taped live is a popular attraction. They often buy a coffee mug in the gift shop, only to bring it home, let it gather dust on a shelf, and then put it out at their next garage sale for as little as a quarter. I have sold the most boring mugs, ones with only the TV show name on them, for $10. I am always happy to pay someone a quarter to take this souvenir off their hands!

Because these mugs tend to only be sold at the actual TV show tapings or at the company stores located in busy tourist areas (such as the NBC store in Times Square in New York City), mugs from both canceled and current shows will sell on Ebay. However, the condition does count, so be sure to check for chips, cracks, and spoon marks.

Several years ago, Target had a bunch of coffee mugs from the television show "The Office" in their $1 section. I bought them all and sold them for $5.99 each, with the buyers paying to ship. Because there were only a few styles, I was able to create one listing for each style with the number of available mugs in each. While the sales of these mugs did not make me rich, they were easy to list (I just took a picture of the front of the mug where the design was) and ship (they fit easily into the 7x7x6 Priority Mail box). And since they were brand new, I did not have to worry about any condition issues.

These days I typically list coffee mugs anywhere from $19.99 to $29.99 and include "free shipping." While mugs tend to be low-dollar sellers, the shipping is typically over a pound once in a shipping box; and that can mean up to $10 for the buyer. I have found that adding the shipping into the price helps move mugs faster as customers are faced with the reality of paying $10 for postage (even though they are).

Ebay has an entire category dedicated to television show coffee mugs (Entertainment Memorabilia – Television Memorabilia – Merchandise & Promotional – Mugs & Coasters). For secondhand mugs, I take pictures of all four sides as well as a picture of the bottom and a picture looking down into the inside of the mug.

We wrap all coffee mugs in bubble wrap and use plenty of packing paper or packing peanuts in the shipping box to ensure they do not break during transit. As I mentioned, mugs fit perfectly into the 7x7x6 Priority Mail boxes, although you will want to make sure you have plain cardboard boxes on hand for mugs shipping via Parcel or internationally.

#89 TV SHOW DVD/ BLU-RAY BOXED SETS

TV show boxed DVD sets can usually be found for cheap at garage sales, and some can bring in great money on Ebay. And while you can charge more for Blu-Ray sets, these are harder to find (but grab them if you do). Since so many people are now switching over from DVD to Blu-Ray, I see more and more DVD box sets at the estate sales I attend for as low as $1.

I have purchased DVD sets brand new to watch myself, and I have been able to make most of my money back on them by reselling them on Ebay after I was done watching them. Not all shows are valuable, though, so do not pay too much; some only go for $9.99 with free shipping, so be sure you leave some room for profit. DVD's are the type of item that makes having a smartphone with internet access helpful as you can check the selling price of them on Ebay before buying them to resell.

Having more than one season of a show to lot together can bring in more money. I recently sold two seasons of "King of the Hill" together for $19.99, while one season of "Columbo" sold for $9.99. Essential each set pieced out to $10 each, but combining more than one set together saves on both listing time and fees as well as shipping costs. I usually offer "free" shipping on media products, building the cost of shipping into the price. To ship one boxed set can cost around $3, while shipping two together may only be $4.

Before purchasing DVD's to resell, make sure the boxes and the discs themselves are in very good condition. There is a lot of competition in the media category, and unless you have a very rare set, the condition is important in order for yours to sell. Cracked cases and scratched disks of basic movies are not going to sell on Ebay. And for sets, be sure all of the disks are included. Unless I know for sure that a DVD will bring in more than $10, I rarely pick up boxed sets for more than $1.

DVDs and Blu-Rays are eligible to ship via Media Mail, but if they are under 16-ounces, you can ship them in a bubble mailer at the First-Class rate for less money (and First Class is much faster than Media, so your customer will be happy). For sets weighing over a pound, we keep a variety of small shipping boxes on hand. While we do buy some plain cardboard shipping boxes from Uline (uline.com), we also save any boxes that we get delivered to our house. Since we sell a wide variety of items on Ebay, we keep a large range of shipping boxes and envelopes on hand so that we always have the right size box at the ready.

Note that we do wrap DVD boxed sets in packing paper. Considering that most come in cardboard sleeves, we take steps to ensure the corners of the boxes don't get dented during shipment. While it is tempting to just toss a DVD set into a bubble mailer, taking a little extra time to wrap, it will go a long way towards pleasing your customer and getting positive feedback.

#90 TYPEWRITER KEYS

I f you ever spot old, antique typewriters for a few bucks, grab them! The condition of the actual typewriter does not matter because it is the keys you want. Crafters, especially jewelry makers, use the glass keys for rings and necklaces. These old models are very heavy and are often rusted, but if the keys are in good shape, you can pull them off and sell them.

We had two such machines that my dad pulled the keys from; together in a lot, the keys sold for $100! Taking the keys off does require some muscle; there are lots of YouTube videos out there to show you how it is done. So many people just toss these clunky typewriters in the trash, so if you are lucky, you may find even find them for free!

While you definitely want to include the number of keys in the lots you are selling, in order to bring in the most money, it is good to put which keys are included, such as the full alphabet and how many numbers. Even though you will be showing the keys in photos, you will likely get questions from potential customers wanting confirmation of what keys are included.

Hauling these heavy typewriters home and then pulling the keys off are the hard parts; photographing, listing, and shipping them is super easy. To photograph, simply lay all of the keys out on a table, taking one picture of all of them together, and then a few more photos of up-close groupings. You may be able to ship these in a Priority Mail Flat Rate Bubble Mailer; just make sure to wrap the keys well in a bag and some packing paper before putting them in the envelope to protect them during transit. If your lot of keys will fit in a Flat Rate envelope, you can simply add $6 to the cost of the lot and offer "free" shipping.

If you find an antique typewriter in good condition, be sure to do a completed listing search on it to determine if you can sell it whole. Note that collectors are extremely picky about these machines being in good condition and that their weight and bulk make shipping them a challenge (you will likely need to ship them via UPS Ground due to their size and weight). However, if you have a typewriter that is in good shape, you may be able to make more money selling it as is. So do your research before pulling the keys and decide if it is worth your time to sell it whole.

#91 UGGS

UGG boots and slippers sell for upwards of $200 new, so finding them secondhand to resell on Ebay is a no-brainer. I do not come across UGGs often, but when I do, and they are in good condition, I will pay $5-10 for them as I can get up to four times that on Ebay.

There are a lot of UGG knock-offs on the market, so be sure you are picking up genuine UGGs to resell on Ebay. UGGs are usually suede with a soft Sherpa lining; they are marked as UGGs on the bottom, on the back heel, and on the inside tag.

Make sure any UGGs you pick up are in good condition. If you plan to be purchasing a lot of shoes to resell on Ebay, it is worth it to invest in some suede and leather cleaners to have on hand to made used shoes look like new. Also, be sure to clean the bottoms of the shoes so that they are free from any dirt. If you feel the insides have a bit of an odor, put a dryer sheet inside of them and put them outside in a shaded area to air out (not in direct sunlight). Putting a bit of time and effort into cleaning any items you are selling on Ebay greatly improves your chances of getting top dollar for them.

In addition to footwear, also look for UGG accessories such as bags. I once found a UGG handbag at Goodwill for $2.50, and I quickly sold it on Ebay for $30. Again, just as UGG shoes are marked as UGG's, UGG bags will be, too.

When listing UGG on Ebay, be sure to take photos off all sides, as well as of the bottoms and the inside label. Since there are counterfeits out there, you want to show customers that you are indeed selling genuine UGGs.

While the Post Office does offer shoe box size Priority Mail boxes, many UGG shoes and most of the boots do not fit inside of these. They do usually fit in the larger 12x12x8 box, though. I offer customers the choice of Parcel Select or Priority for most items I list on Ebay, including shoes. If they choose Parcel, I will still check to see what Priority costs as with the online shipping discount, and Priority is almost always less than Parcel for items under four pounds.

Since shoes and boots are not going to break during shipment, you do not have to go overboard with packing materials. Many sellers put shoes in large plastic bags and then use some packing paper or peanuts to surround the shoes in the box to prevent them from bouncing around during transit. Depending on the price I am asking, I may or may not offer "free" shipping on Uggs. If they are a particularly expensive pair, I will often add the shipping into the price. However, for a pair going for $25-50, I will use calculated shipping and have the buyer pay the shipping cost.

#92 VESTS

I mentioned earlier in this book that puffer vests sell well on Ebay, but it is worth noting that vests of all styles are usually good sellers, too. I have sold almost every kind of vest, including pull-over sweater vests, buttoned sweater vest cardigans, vests meant to go under suits, vests that act as lightweight jackets, and casual business vests that are worn over blouses.

My Goodwill stores have racks specifically designated for vests, and I always make sure to look through them for good brand names. However, I also check the coat and blazer sections as sometimes they put vests there, too.

Denim and corduroy vests from good brands (Gap, Levi, Lee) are usually an easy $30 sale on Ebay. I also pick up dressier vests from the nicer mall stores such as Banana Republic, Coldwater Creek, and Talbots. While I generally stick to larger sizes when it comes to the clothes I sell on Ebay, I will buy vests in smaller sizes to resell if they are from a better brand name. In addition to the brands I have already named, I have also sold vests from Calvin Klein, Lauren by Ralph Lauren, J. Crew, and L.L. Bean for as much as $40.

Listing vests on Ebay is very easy. I take four photos: one of the front-side, one of the back-side, one of the collar-tag, and one of the arm-hole. For measurements, I provide the armpit-to-armpit and length. I also make sure to list the material, any pockets, and whether the piece has buttons or zippers. While buyers can see most of these details in the photos, it is always good to write them out. Providing as much information as you can in your Ebay listings protects you from buyers coming back claiming you misrepresented what you sold and demanding a refund.

Vests are usually lightweight enough to ship in a poly mailer at the First-Class postage rate. Because of this, vests are usually an item I list with "free" shipping as it is easy to add a few dollars into the price to cover the postage.

#93 VICTORIA'S SECRET BAGS

Victoria's Secret products are rather pricey and have a large fan base, so they have a nice resale value on Ebay. In addition to bras, sleepwear, and beauty products, all being good items to pick up to resell, also snag any Victoria Secret bags you may find.

Victoria's Secret often offers free or discount gift with purchase items that come in branded bags. These bags can be as elaborate as actual purses or as simple as lightweight cotton reusable totes. Many have PINK printed on them, which is Victoria's Secret most popular line of products. While I have sold Pink branded purses for around $20, some older styles can bring over $100 on Ebay!

Many women who get these bags are only after the products inside, so the bag gets put out at their own garage sale or sent to the thrift store, often still with their tags on. New bags with tags will bring in the most money, but even bags without their tags and those that are gently used will sell as long as they are in good condition.

These bags are another easy item to list on Ebay as you only need to take a photo of the front, one photo of the back-side, and one phone on the inside of the bag. You will want to give the measurements, too. Be sure to describe the condition accurately;

do not list an item as new just because you do not think it was used. If the hangtag is missing, but the bag looks new, list it as "used," but in the listing, put something like "without tag but doesn't appear to have ever been used." Always understate the condition of the secondhand items you sell on Ebay to protect yourself from a buyer filing a claim against you, saying you misrepresented something.

When listing anything fabric on Ebay, it is important to note whether it is from a smoker's home. While you may not know the origin of the bags you pick up, if you are a non-smoker, you will likely be able to tell right away if an item was near smoke. Some people are extremely sensitive to smoke, so if you are not able to detect smells on your own, enlist a non-smoking friend or family member to give items a whiff. Items from a smoker's home will still sell, but you need to disclose that in the listing. I also air out items by putting a scented dryer sheet inside of them and putting them outside in the shade for a day.

As with most clothing, Victoria's Secret bags are rather lightweight and can ship in a polybag. If they weigh under 16 ounces, they can ship via First Class. Heavier bags will need to go via Parcel or Priority, and as I have said numerous times in this book, Priority is often less than Parcel with the Ebay shipping discount. To avoid adding extra weight to shipments by using a Priority Mail box, however, we put bags into poly mailers and then put Priority Mail stickers on the outside. This way, the package ships via Priority Mail but without having to add a pound to the cost of postage due to the box.

Victoria's Secret is also popular internationally, so you will want to list these items using Ebay's Global Shipping Program. When an international customer buys from you through the Global Shipping Program, you simply package and ship the item to the Ebay distribution center, where they will then handle the customs forms and labeling needed to send the package overseas. The address for the distribution center will automatically be added to the customer's order; you just print your label as you would for any other customer. You do not have to change anything on your end. This makes shipping to customers all over the world fast and easy!

#94 VINTAGE CAMERAS

Cameras are another favorite item of mine to resell on Ebay BUT one I am very careful not to overpay for. Sometimes the most interesting looking cameras are worth the least, while a little ho-hum model is the one to bring in the big money. I do not like paying more than a dollar or two for a camera unless I am absolutely sure I know its value.

The older cameras are usually the best sellers on Ebay as collectors buy them. However, if you can get newer models super cheap, you may be able to put a lot of them together for parts. Cameras are an item I sell "as is" since there is usually no way for me to test them. Camera collectors are very particular, so do not over-state the condition. However, if you are able to determine that a camera is in working condition, you will get top dollar for it.

One of my best camera sales I ever had was a dirty old camera I found at a garage sale. I found it in the back of the garage, and it was covered with dust and dead bugs. I paid $2 for it, and it sold on Ebay for $100! I also regularly pick up Polaroid cameras at estate sales for under $5 that, untested, are usually a quick $40 sale on Ebay.

The Ebay "Sold" completed listings for vintage cameras is another category you should take the time to study. There have been so many different styles and models of cameras released over the years; it is very easy to have two that look relatively the same, but one could actually be worthless while the other is a rare issue.

Before listing a camera on Ebay, I do a completed listing search on it to see what the going rate for it is. I then list it as Fixed Price with the buyer paying shipping. Usually, cameras are small enough to fit into the Priority Mail 7x7x6 boxes; and we use plenty of bubble wrap to protect them during transit.

For the listing itself, I take photos of all sides as well as the bottom. I also copy any information printed on the camera into the item description field. This is also where I will add that the camera is untested and is being sold "as is."

#95 VINTAGE CAMERA FILM & FLASH BULBS

A long with selling vintage cameras on Ebay, I am also always on the lookout for camera accessories, especially unused film and flashbulbs. Again, the older, the better on these items as you are selling to collectors desperate to get their hands-on products no longer made.

I like to lot loose film and bulbs together as they are so much easier to list and ship. If there are no boxes for the bulbs, it can be hard to accurately describe what they are; I always take lots of good, up-close photographs. I always list these "as-is" to ensure a customer does not come back, claiming I promised products that end up not working.

You will want to note the expiration date listed on the box of any film you sell. Of course, since the film is old, the expiration dates are always long overdue; but that does not stop die-hard photographers from paying top dollar for them. Especially hot is Polaroid film.

While I generally stick to listing items at Fixed Price on Ebay, vintage film and bulbs are items I will sometimes take a chance on at auction, especially if I have a mixed lot of different brands and sizes. Since I am usually able to pick up film and bulbs at estate sales for a quarter, these are fun items to try at auction that also bring traffic to my other listings. I normally start these auctions out at $9.99, with the buyer paying shipping. I use calculated shipping so that the buyer pays the exact postage cost to their zip code.

The tried-and-true 7x7x6 Priority Mail box is great for shipping small lots of film or bulbs. Rarely does the box end up weighing more than a pound, but be sure to get a weight before you list to ensure you do not lose money on the shipping. Take care to wrap loose bulbs so that they do not break during transit.

#96 VINTAGE DOONEY & BOURKE

Buying designer purses at garage sales and thrift stores is very risky because they are so many fakes out there, especially on mid-level designer names such as Coach. I actually no longer buy designer bags secondhand to resell on Ebay as I have gotten burned a few times accidentally picking up fakes. Ebay scours the site for counterfeit goods, so do not even think of trying to list a fake bag on Ebay as it will get taken down. And if you are found to repeatedly be doing this, Ebay can suspend your account.

One designer brand I will pick up, however, is vintage Dooney & Bourke. While the newer bags and wallets are susceptible to being knocked off, the vintage bags are not. Vintage Dooney & Bourke products are usually green or blue with brown trim and a brown leather circle patch on the front. The patch features a duck surrounded by the words "Dooney & Bourke All Weather Leather."

My last Dooney & Bourke sale was a small wallet that I paid $5 for at an estate sale; it sold quickly on Ebay for $25. An actual vintage Dooney & Bourke purse can sell for hundreds of dollars on Ebay, depending on the age, style, and condition. And the condition is very important; a ripped bag is not going to sell. Fortunately, these pieces are made from high-quality leather and usually hold up extremely well.

As I have mentioned several times throughout this book, it is worth your time to study the completed listings of items on Ebay. Take a few minutes to scroll through the "Sold" section of the completed listings for "vintage Dooney & Bourke" on Ebay to familiarize yourself with what to look out for.

And if you do end up buying a vintage Dooney & Bourke bag to list on Ebay, be sure to take photos from the piece from all sides, as well as the bottom and a picture of the inside. Include the measurements both in the item specific fields as well as in the description (because even though you fill out the item specifics, some people do not see them and will ask for more details). For any purse you list on Ebay, you will want to provide the height, length, and depth.

Because of their size and bulk, we usually wrap bags in bubble wrap before putting them in a large poly mailing bag. I then check the difference between Parcel Select and Priority Mail. If Priority is less or only a bit more, I will ship via Priority and just add Priority stickers to the outside of the polybag. Smaller items such as wallets, key chains, and checkbook covers fit easily into bubble mailers and can usually ship via First Class Mail as they are under 16 ounces.

#97 VINTAGE PORTABLE TYPEWRITERS

Portable typewriters (i.e., manual and non-electric) are one of my favorite things to pick up to sell on Ebay. Usually, they come in fun retro colors such as eggshell blue or mint green. Pink and red units are rare and especially desirable.

Collectors LOVE these typewriters as they look fabulous just as a display piece. Sometimes I luck out and find these with their original cases, but they will still sell without them. Note that I am referring to typewriters with a plastic color case on them; these are different than the antique all-metal typewriters I talked about in terms of pulling their keys off to resell. Some people who buy these typewriters plan to actually use them for typing as they prefer the old-fashioned method over using a computer.

Smith Corona and Royal are the two most common brands of vintage typewriters you will likely come across when at thrift stores, garage sales, and estate sales. I find these all of the time on the floors of estate sales, usually pushed back into a corner as people do not know their value. The most I have ever paid for one of these is $15, but I am usually able to pick them up for

$5. The last one I bought sold for $99.99 with the buyer paying shipping.

As with anything that serious collectors are after, I am very careful to list portable typewriters "as is." While they may seem to type fine for me, I need to protect myself against someone saying a miscellaneous part inside of the unit does not work. Most of these typewriters will need new ribbons due to age; again, that is part of the "as is" condition. However, the ribbons being dried out does not deter collectors are they understand these dry out over time.

These typewrites are heavy and bulky, so I also have the buyer pay the shipping cost using the calculated shipping feature on Ebay. We almost always ship typewriters via Parcel Select, and we made sure we have a cardboard box on hand before I even list it, so we will be ready to ship when it sells. My dad uses plenty of bubble wrap along with packing paper and peanuts to ensure these typewriters arrive at their destination intact.

#98 WATKINS
CERAMIC PIE PLATES

I f you are a frequent thrift store and garage sale shopper, you have likely seen ceramic pie plates with a color illustration of a pie, and the recipe for it printed on the inside bottom. Always turn these plates over to see if there are from Wilton and if they are, and you can get them cheap, pick them up to sell on Ebay.

These pie plates are not big moneymakers; they average between $15 and $20, depending on the version. However, I can usually pick them up for around a dollar, so they are a nice addition to my Ebay store inventory.

With all ceramics, I make sure to thoroughly look them over for any chips, cracks, or scratches. Often these pie plates were simply used for decoration, not baking, so often they are in very good condition.

Watkins pie plates are easy to list as you only need to provide a photograph of the front and one of the back as well as the diameter and the depth. I also copy whatever markings are on the bottom of the plate into the listing (usually, these will have a year and a country of the manufacturer printed on them).

Since these plates are heavy, lower-cost items, I list them using calculated shipping so that the buyer pays the postage cost based on their location. I have sold these plates for $15 to buyers who have had to pay $15 to have them shipped. However, they were collectors who were happy to pay the price.

Even though these pie plates are not very deep and could probably go in a flatter rectangular box, we still usually ship them in the 12x12x8 Priority Mail box, using lots of bubble wrap and packing paper to make sure the plate does not break in transit.

#99 WILTON
CAKE PANS

I love finding aluminum Wilton cake pans to resell on Ebay. Whether they are shaped like cartoon characters or are holiday-themed, they have consistently been a great seller for me over the years. I often find these pans at estate sales where they are usually dusty and dirty, and I usually only pay $1 for them. We have spent a lot of time over the years washing these cake pans up to bring them back to sellable condition!

I love to find these pans with their original paper inlays that feature a color photo of the finished cake along with decorating tips, but the pans will still sell without these paper inserts. If the pan was used, it would almost likely have scratches. And since the older pans were made of lightweight aluminum (today they are much heavier and sturdier), it is not unusual for them to have some dents and to not even lay flat. Customers will still purchase pans that are not perfect; just make sure to accurately describe any condition issues in your listing and to provide several good photographs.

Each of these pans is stamped with a model number on the back, so be sure to include that in your listing. Also, provide the pan's measurements (length, width, and height). Putting these details into your listing will cut down on questions from potential customers.

Many of these cake pans will sell on their own, although, because they are rather large and bulky, the shipping usually equals the price of the pan. Therefore, I like to put several of these pans together in one lot as bakers are looking to get several at once to add to the catalog of cake shapes and designs that they can offer their customers.

I always do a completed listing search on each pan to see if it will sell on its own. There are some rare Disney and Teenage Mutant Ninja Turtle pans, for example, that can bring in as much as $75 each, but usually, most pans are in the $15 range.

I recently sold a lot of eight pans for $60, and the buyer paid the shipping. These pans are usually too big to fit into any of the Priority Mail boxes; so, you will need a large, plain cardboard box for shipping. I always make sure to have the box ready before I list these pans so that I am not scrambling to find one when they ship.

Selling several pans together usually means the box will be over the Priority Mail size limit, so plan on shipping lots via Parcel Post. My dad wraps each pan in a sheet of bubble wrap to protect the pans from banging against one another during transit.

#100 WOOLRICH CLOTHING

T he Woolrich brand was founded in 1830 and is the oldest manufacturer of outdoor wear in America. Today, most of their manufacturing is done overseas, although some garments and much of the woolen fabrics are still made in the U.S.A. Woolrich produces clothing for both men and women with an emphasis on work and outdoor pieces.

Vintage Woolrich is easy to spot as the label will read "Made in the U.S.A." Their thick, flannel men's shirts sell extremely well on Ebay; larger sizes in excellent condition can go for as much as $75. However, the average selling price for Woolrich clothing on Ebay is $35, which is not a bad profit considering I can easily find these pieces at Goodwill for as little as $1.

For the modern Woolrich pieces (identifiable because they are NOT made in the U.S.A.), I stick to sizes large or bigger. Extra-large and up-sell extremely well in both men's and women's; although overall, the men's clothing sells better than the women's does. Before buying any piece of clothing, including Woolrich, be sure to look the piece over for stains or rips; and check the buttons to make sure they are all intact. Also, make sure the size tag has not been cut out.

I have mentioned before that we wash all clothing before listing it on Ebay. I take three photos of shirts: front, back, and an up-close shot of the collar/tag area. I provide three measurements in all shirt and coat listings, taken by laying the garment flat out on a table: pit to pit (tape measure drawn from under one armpit to the other), sleeve (tape measure drawn from the shoulder seam to the cuff; or from the collar to the cuff if there is no seam), and body length (tape measure drawn from the collar to the hem).

Woolrich flannel shirts tend to be heavy; therefore, they often need to be shipped at the one to two-pound rate. This is where Priority Mail Flat Rate Bubble Mailers come in handy as I can ship these shirts for under $6 anywhere in the country. To get bulky clothes into the bubble mailers, we roll them up and put them in a polybag. The polybag then slides easily into the bubble mailer. Without the polybag, the bubbles inside of the envelope tend to stick to the clothing fabric, making it difficult to get the garment inside on its own.

#101 WORKOUT TAPES & DVDS

S o many people buy workout DVDs with every intention of using them, only to play them once, if at all. That is why they are in abundance at garage sales, usually for less than a dollar. But just because one person did not want these does not mean someone else is not looking for them; so, workout tapes and DVD's sell great on Ebay.

Wait, did I just say tapes? As in, VHS tapes? Yup, old VHS tapes of workouts featuring Jane Fonda or other fitness gurus of the 1980s can easily sell on their own for an average of $10, more for a lot of several together. Since you can usually pick these tapes up for a quarter at thrift stores and garage sales, they are great to grab and save up until you have a few to sell together.

And while vintage VHS fitness tapes are a fun pick up, modern fitness DVD's are even better as they sell for more. Take a look at the completed listings on Ebay, and you will see that some single DVD's can sell for as much as $100! Even basic disks from relatively unknown teachers sell well. I recently sold three workout DVDs for $18 that I had paid 75-cents for at a garage sale.

While you may not be able to test VHS tapes (unless you have a VHS player), you can look over DVD disks to ensure they are not scratched. Note that some of these DVD's were originally sold

ANN ECKHART

with stretch bands or other accessories, so be sure to check for
all of the pieces. If the extras are not included with the DVD, the
disks can still sell. However, you want to make sure customers
know exactly what they are buying, so be very clear in your Ebay
listing of what exactly is and is not included.

Workout VHS tapes and DVD disks qualify for Media Mail and
slide easily into bubble mailers. If a disk weighs less than 16-
ounces, you will likely be able to ship it via First Class for less
than Media Mail, which means your customer will receive their
order much faster. For multiple tapes and disks, check to see
what the Parcel and Priority Mail rates are compared to Media
Mail. While Media Mail is cheap, it is also super slow; anytime
I am able to afford to upgrade an order to a faster shipping
method, I will.

CONCLUSION

So, there you have it: 101 items that you should be able to easily find at garage sales and thrift stores to resell on Ebay! I hope you found this list helpful and that you are able to make some MONEY from the tips I have given you. And for even more things to sell on Ebay, check out the sequel to this book, "101 MORE Items to Sell on Ebay" on Amazon (here is the link to my Amazon Author Page for all of my titles: https://amzn.to/2njSMw5

Remember, too, that a lot of things factor into a successful Ebay sale. Your feedback rating, quality of photos, shipping charges, item condition, competition, and current demand all determine the price you will get. Before listing any item on Ebay, be sure to do a completed listing search to see what the going rate for yours is. While these are my own personal success stories, what sells today may not sell tomorrow as the Ebay market is constantly changing.

Selling on Ebay, while fun and profitable, is work. The harder you work, the more money you will make!

Looking for more help with growing your Ebay business? Be sure to check out my other reselling books, all of which are available on Amazon on both Kindle and in paperback.

ABOUT THE AUTHOR

Ann Eckhart is a writer, reseller, and online content creator based in Iowa. She has numerous books available about how to make money online and from home. Check out her Amazon Author Page at https://amzn.to/34nE9us for all her titles.

You can keep up with everything Ann does on her blog at www.AnnEckhart.com. You can also connect with her on the following social media networks:

FACEBOOK: https://www.facebook.com/anneckhart/

TWITTER: https://twitter.com/ann_eckhart

INSTAGRAM: https://www.instagram.com/ann_eckhart/

YOUTUBE RESELLING CHANNEL: https://tinyurl.com/yxvqtwc7

YOUTUBE VLOG CHANNEL: https://tinyurl.com/yxjqn6d2